HUMBLED BY THESE WORDS . . .

The team chaplain at a major Power Five school might be one of the most important staff members in the program. There's always a time when players need to talk to someone besides their position coach or head coach, and the team chaplain can stand in the gap during those moments. Thomas Settles did a wonderful job doing just that. The weekly team chapel before each game was always a time to help me center my thoughts on the things that were the most important, and that is my relationship with Jesus Christ!

If you would like to get an inside look at what goes on just hours before kickoff, this book will be fun and informative. And who knows, it just may change your life!

- Mark Richt
Former Head Football Coach, The University of Georgia, and The University of Miami, 2023 College Football Hall of Fame inductee

Thomas Settles is a tangible example of a father, a pastor, and a man for me. As his first disciple at the University of Georgia , he showed me the impact of being a spiritual leader in the locker room. He has prayed with me before every game I played in the NFL over my 9-year career. He answers my calls no matter how late or how early it may be. He is a perfect reflection of what consistent faith looks like through mountain top and valley experiences. He taught me to always stand on the foundation of the word of God in all moments of my life.

-Fernando Velasco
University of Georgia Football Letterman, 9-year NFL veteran, Director of Player Engagement for The Atlanta Falcons

The pre-game chapels set my eyes on Christ and allow for reflection. It helps me to realize that the Glory is never mine and it belongs to God.

-Sedrick Van Pran
UGA Letterman and 2022 UGA Football Captain

With our rigorous schedules, pre-game chapel and bible study were vital for my faith. As a college athlete, many things can distract you from what is most important. T-Sett committed to teaching me and others about the Word of God. He welcomed us to services and was always available to discuss our faith.

-Andrew Thomas
UGA Letterman and 4th overall pick of the 2020 NFL draft

Thomas always did a tremendous job of making sure we all understood the bigger picture of why God put us in the position we were as a student-athlete at UGA. As football players we get so focused on the game and what we need to do to make sure our bodies are properly prepared each week. T-Set had this natural ability to bring us the scripture in a way that reminded me that there is more to life than just ball.

-Aaron Murray
UGA letterman, NFL Veteran, and Network Sports Analyst

I love Thomas Settles. There are many reasons why but the biggest is that we both love Jesus and want others to know His love.

-Jeff Foxworthy
Comedian, Actor, Host, Author

ACKNOWLEDGMENTS

Now unto Him who is able to do exceedingly abundantly above all that we ask or think, according to the power that works in us, 21 to Him be glory in the church by Christ Jesus to all generations, forever and ever. Amen.
- **Ephesians 3:20-21**

As long as I can remember I have held the firm conviction that the Lord has been better to me than I deserve, and He has always exceeded my expectations. When I think about the family God allowed me to be birthed into; when I think about the people who have invested in me throughout my life; when I consider the family that I have, the church that I pastor, and the ministry on campus that I lead, all of those are just reminders of God's grace to me, and this book is simply the newest reminder.

"Better Together" is not an opportunity for me to preach to people, but it is an opportunity for me to humbly share how God has challenged me and encouraged me in my faith. Simply put, this book is an overflow of how God challenged me during the fall of 2021, and I pray that it challenges and encourages you in your walk with Christ.

Before you begin reading, I would like to take the time to acknowledge a few people.

To my parents, Thomas Settles and Sandra Stanley Perkins, thank you for always praying for me, believing in me, and supporting me. To all of my donors, supporters, and board members, thank you for investing in the ministry and opening a door for me to serve. To my creative team, Adam Beane, Larry and Betty Chapman, Jake Baker, Andy Johnston, and Avita Settles, I really can't thank you all enough for helping this project become a reality.

To my amazing wife, my co-laborer for life, Avita thank you for always supporting me, encouraging me, and trusting me to lead our family. You are a tremendous gift from God, and I'm honored to do life with you.

Last but not least, I want to thank the Lord. On December 2, 1996, I placed my faith in Christ. On that day, I didn't fully understand what that meant, but I'm thankful that the Holy Spirit revealed my need for Christ and is allowing me to grow in grace. Following Jesus has taken me to places that I could have never imagined, and I can honestly say that it is a privilege to serve Him.

— *Thomas C. Settles, III*

ABOUT THE AUTHOR

Thomas C. Settles, III is the Senior Pastor of Calvary Bible Church and also serves as the FCA Campus Director for the University of Georgia. He was born and raised in Chattanooga, Tennessee, and surrendered his life to Christ as a 15-year-old. At age 20, he committed to full-time Christian ministry during his undergraduate sophomore year at Morehouse College, in Atlanta, Georgia.

Upon graduating from Morehouse College in 2003, Thomas enrolled at Beeson Divinity School of Samford University in Birmingham, Alabama, and received his Master of Divinity.

After completing his studies at Beeson, Thomas moved to Athens, Georgia and he considers the Classic City to be home.

Thomas has a tremendous love for discipleship through the local church and is excited about equipping believers to go outside of the four walls of the church to do the work of the ministry. Thomas is a supervising member of the University Religious Life Association at UGA and serves on the Board of directors for The Food Bank of Northeast Georgia and Downtown Ministries.

Thomas is married to Avita, his wife and "co-laborer for life" of over 10 years. They are the grateful parents of four gifts from God.

BETTER
TOGETHER

FIFTEEN ENCOURAGING MESSAGES FROM AN
UNFORGETTABLE 2021 SEASON

A DEVOTIONAL BY
THOMAS C. SETTLES, III

ISBN 9798868121227
First paperback edition December 2023.
Cover photo credit: The Late Terry "Big Dog" Stephens

Edited by Adan Beane
Cover art and layout by A.Y. Settles

Kindle Direct Publishing

BETTER TOGETHER

FIFTEEN ENCOURAGING MESSAGES FROM AN UNFORGETTABLE 2021 SEASON

TABLE OF CONTENTS:

WEEK 1	MINDSET: WE ARE BETTER TOGETHER	1
WEEK 2	KNOWING WHY	11
WEEK 3	TOUGHNESS	20
WEEK 4	COMPOSURE	29
WEEK 5	RESILIENCY	38
WEEK 6	DEMAND THE STANDARD	46
WEEK 7	SELF TALK	55
WEEK 8	HELP OTHERS WIN	65
WEEK 9	HUMILITY	73
WEEK 10	BELIEVE	81
WEEK 11	MISTAKES: THE DANGER OF DRIFTING	89
WEEK 12	ACCOUNTABILITY	97
WEEK 13	GRATITUDE	106
WEEK 14	NEXT LEVEL: HOLD THE LADDER	113
WEEK 15	BEAT AS ONE	122

CHAPTER 1
MINDSET: WE ARE BETTER TOGETHER

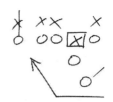

ATHENS, GA
SEPTEMBER 4, 2021

12 For just as the body is one and has many members, and all the members of the body, though many, are one body, so it is with Christ. 13 For in one Spirit we were all baptized into one body—Jews or Greeks, slaves or free—and all were made to drink of one Spirit. 14 For the body does not consist of one member but of many. 15 If the foot should say, "Because I am not a hand, I do not belong to the body," that would not make it any less a part of the body. 16 And if the ear should say, "Because I am not an eye, I do not belong to the body," that would not make it any less a part of the body. 17 If the whole body were an eye, where would be the sense of hearing? If the whole body were an ear, where would be the sense of smell? 18 But as it is, God arranged the members in the body, each one of them, as he chose. 19 If all were a single member, where would the body be? 20 As it is, there are many parts, yet one body. 21 The eye cannot say to the hand, "I have no need of you," nor again the head to the feet, "I have no need of you." 22 On the contrary, the parts of the body that seem to be weaker are indispensable, 23 and on those parts of the body that we think less honorable we bestow the greater honor, and our unpresentable parts are treated with greater modesty, 24 which our more presentable parts do not require. But God has so composed the body, giving greater honor to the part that lacked it, 25 that there may be no division in the body, but that the members may have the same care for one another.
1 Corinthians 12:12-25

Mt. Everest is known as the highest mountain in the world. Its highest point is 29,000 feet above sea level, and it was not until 1953 that a person reached the top of the mountain. The name Edmund Hillary probably doesn't sound familiar to you, but he is credited as the first man to make it to the top of Mt. Everest. Now, while it is true that Hillary was the first to make it to the summit, what is also true is the fact that he didn't get there alone. When you research the events leading up to Hillary making it to the top of the mountain, you will find that there was a mountain tour guide named Tenzing Norgay who showed Hillary the path to get to the top. Tenzing was from a local village at the bottom of the mountain. Now, I want you to catch this: Tenzing had more skill than Hillary. Tenzing had more experience than Hillary. Tenzing knew the route better than Hilliary. Even during one of the early stages of the climb, Hillary fell while trying to scale a wall, and Tenzing had to save his life. What is most interesting about the story is when asked why he allowed Hillary to reach the summit first, Tenzing responded, "I didn't want to make it to the top alone." Pause for a second and think about how powerful that statement is, "I didn't want to make it to the top alone. " Brothers and sisters, just dream with me for a second. How great could we be this season if we adopted that mindset? Family, what could we accomplish this year if we all had the mindset, "I don't want to make it to the top alone."? Just saying that gets me excited! Not just simply for a football game, but it gets me excited about what we can accomplish in the classroom. What we can achieve on our campus and back in our hometowns excites me. Tenzing was communicating that reaching the top with a brother was more important than reaching the top alone. Think for a second. How different would you be if you adopted that mentality? How much more impactful could your life be if you possessed that mindset?

That story reminds me of God's desire for us! Please don't miss this. The journey we are starting today, this brand new season, gives us an opportunity to live out that mindset. As we live out our faith, we are invited to experience the kind of relationship where we refuse to live life alone. When I think about the story and the scripture passage, I am reminded of one of God's greatest blessings to us.

When we place our faith in Christ, God places His spirit inside us. We are adopted into the family of God. Therefore, we're not only given an eternal home in heaven, but we become a spiritual family member. Many don't realize it, but God has blessed us with brothers and sisters in Christ.

Most of the time, we think of material things when we conceive of blessings. We think about the house. We think about the car. We think about a more prominent promotion or a more significant title.

I concede that while these are all great gifts, God's greatest gifts are to be experienced in doing life with other people.

Let me just say to you, brothers and sisters, you all are a blessing to me. I'm thankful when I think about all the people God has placed in my life. When I look around the rooms God allows me to be present in, I see a room full of blessings. I see people who have overcome adversity. I see people who have prayed for me. I see folks who have supported me. I see people who others have counted out, but who are people who, by the power of God, are doing great and mighty things! If you don't receive anything else in this devotional, don't miss this:

One of God's greatest blessings for your life is the people He has planted in your life.

Our brothers and sisters in Christ are a blessing! We are indeed better together. I want you to hear my heart on this one - We are better together, and our mindset should be: I don't want to get to the top alone. It doesn't matter how much talent I have. It doesn't matter how many stars I had in high school. My draft grade doesn't matter.

How much NIL money I have received doesn't matter. What matters most is that I grow to become the man or woman God calls me to be. That is the mindset that God is inviting us to accept. God invites us to embrace the idea that we are not meant to do it alone, not even a coach, a professor, or even a parent, but God tells us that whatever we do, we should do it with others. That is what our text is communicating. It reminds us of an often-neglected blessing from God.

Megastar comedian and actor Kevin Hart tells the story about neglecting to take advantage of a blessing that his mom sent him. We know him as a success now, but Kevin Hart was a struggling actor and stand-up comic for many years. He didn't have much money and certainly didn't have many opportunities. While struggling, his mom sent him a Bible and encouraged him to read it. Initially, he blew it off. He thought, "Man, I don't need no Bible." Conventional wisdom told him that he needed money. He needed movie industry connections. He thought what he needed could only be found outside of the Bible.

Whenever he spoke to his mom, she asked if he had read his Bible. I'm sure a couple of you reading this devotional have heard that same question from a parent. So, to get her off his back, Kevin finally decided to open up the Bible. And when he did, he found that his mother had placed money inside the book. I wouldn't be surprised if some of you look for some money inside your Bible this week! Here is the point I'm trying to make: sometimes, in life, God will give you precisely what you need, but sometimes, it comes in a way you don't expect. I know you think you need "more playing time," but what if what you need most is to humble yourself and support the team? I know you want more touches, but what if you really need to pay more attention to details to help the team? I know you want to make it to the next level, but maybe you need to learn what it looks like to be faithful on this level.

The Bible speaks about the blessing of community and how it is often neglected. In the text, God communicates that He has a lot of work for you to do. He says there's a lot to be accomplished. But the passage is also telling us that the fullness of what God wants us to experience cannot be done alone. Yes, there are many blessings that God will give you that you can enjoy by yourself, but for this one, you will need others, brothers and sisters, walking alongside you in your life.

Let's give some background to the passage. The Corinthian church was special and unique. Its members were extremely gifted. Think of it this way: if there was a church that was ever full of 5-star recruits, then it was this church. In fact, they were so gifted that their giftedness led them to selfishness. They were so gifted that they all wanted to be Lead Dawg. They were so gifted they thought they should be the center of attention. They were so gifted that they lost sight of the mission and the vision they had received from the Lord. Rather than doing things God's way, they acted like many of us and decided to do things their own way.

The Apostle Paul, in order to remind them of the mission, gives them a lesson on the importance of biblical brotherhood. He reminds them that being a Christian means they are now a part of God's family. He communicated that once they signed those spiritual scholarship papers, they acknowledged that what was best for the team had to be more important than what was best for them. Upon signing those spiritual scholarship papers, they had to realize that they had to do things God's way to experience God's best. The Apostle Paul tells them three things about biblical community that I believe also apply to any believer today:

1. The Blessing of a Brotherhood

13 For in one Spirit we were all baptized into one body...

In verse 13, we have a term in the word 'baptism' that often gets confusing for believers. Just so we are on the same page, baptism is an outward sign of an inward change. When a person is baptized, the preacher submerges them in water, and they are laid flat. Being laid down flat is to simulate the act of one dying. And being raised from the water is a picture of a new person being born again. Baptism is a critical practice, reminding us of where we should place our identity. As a believer, my identity is in Christ. Beyond what I can or cannot do, God determines my identity.

As a chaplain, my phone rings more often during two specific times of the year. The first time is in the spring, right after the NFL draft. The second time is right about now, during the beginning of fall, when teams make their final cut, narrowing down their rosters to 53. I'm not making light of this truth, but I'd invite you to consider the following: If your dream is to make it to the NFL, what happens if your name doesn't get called? If your name gets called, what happens when you don't get drafted in the expected round? What happens when your time is up and you get cut? Let's take it out of the realm of sports - what happens when you don't have the career you expected? Or the family you desired or the lifestyle you envisioned?

When life doesn't play out how we expect, it usually causes us to ask," Who am I?" For many young men, we've been living and breathing football since childhood. It's all we know. Our identity is tied to the gridiron. What happens when football is over? This is true with this sport and in any area of life. What you do *must* be separated from who you are.

Many of you know I've been doing a unique ministry in Athens, GA, since 2007. By the grace of God, I hope I will still be doing ministry here in Athens in 2057. But there will come a day and time when another minister is in my role. Currently, I serve as the pastor of Calvary Bible Church. I love our church community, but there will be another pastor eventually. So, if I place my identity in what I do, what happens when what I do changes?

If you place your identity in what you do on the football field or in your vocational job, what will happen when you can no longer be on the field? Or what if you don't get on the field as much as you want? What happens when you get on the field, and it doesn't go the way you expect? What happens when you don't get the job? Or when your career isn't on the fast track? How will you handle it when you can't take the vacation you dreamed of or don't have the family you prayed for?

The reality is that we are called to be a part of something so much bigger than ourselves. This means that my identity should be found there, not in a field or a job. The text first mentions being baptized by the Spirit, meaning you belong to Christ's body. Secondly, it says being filled with the Spirit, meaning that our bodies belong to Christ. I know you are a part of the team or a family, but the question is whether the team or the family has all of you.

We have a phenomenal football team here in Athens, GA and it's a privilege to be a dawg. Now, it's one thing to wear the G, but it's another thing to belong to the G. Whenever the team leaves Athens, the players get to enjoy the plane. They get to eat the meals and partake in the late-night snacks. There are many things that the players "get to receive," but the best players don't simply focus on what they get from the team. They focus on what the team receives from them. The best players on the team consider whether the team got consistent sleep during the week. Did the team give their best effort in the weight room? Did the team get some extra time in the film study? It's one thing to get something from the team, but the question a good teammate considers is – what did the team get from me?

If we can understand that principle concerning a team, how much more should we appreciate what is being communicated in the text? Since God has been gracious to me and has invited me into a community, I don't simply want to receive from the brotherhood, but I should wish to be a blessing to the brotherhood. No, we cannot repay God for our salvation. Likewise, our relationship with God is not marked by our performance (church attendance, reading the Bible, etc.), evaluating what we do and don't do, and constantly deciding whether He wants to bless or strike us down. None of that is the case. However, God does want us to trust Him. God is not waiting for our performance to impress Him, but He desires that we simply put our faith in Him. One of the ways that we trust Him is by honoring and serving Him. God certainly wants to bless us as members of His body, but He also wants to make us a blessing as a member of His body!

2. The Beauty of a Brotherhood

16 And if the ear should say, "Because I am not an eye, I do not belong to the body," that would not make it any less a part of the body. 17 If the whole body were an eye, where would be the sense of hearing? If the whole body were an ear, where would be the sense of smell? 18 But as it is, God arranged the members in the body, each one of them, as he chose. 19 If all were a single member, where would the body be? 20 As it is, there are many parts, yet one body.

Let me ask you a question: when you look at your life, who benefits the most by your presence? Think of it this way: let's say you got to be a part of your favorite sports team, and you had the opportunity to travel with that team to a big game; who would benefit most by you being there? Take some time and think about that question.
Whatever team you are on or whatever family you belong to - do you get more than they receive? It's a give-and-take relationship - where do you land? Do you give more than you receive?

God wants you to benefit from being a part of a community! No question. But if you are the only one who benefits, that is not true success. If things have to be done according to your timetable, then the team, family, or community will not experience success. As we grow in our relationship with God, we must do the hard work to remember that we belong to something much bigger than ourselves.

Do you know the quickest way to neutralize a part of your body? Whether it be an arm or a leg, the fastest way to render a part of the body ineffectual and useless is to sever it from the rest of the body. When I do my own thing, I am actively deciding to cut myself off from the body. When I am unwilling to serve or consider others better than myself, I am cutting myself off from the body. More to the point, I'm hurting myself *and* the body. Both are in worse shape without one another. If we can understand that to be accurate, we can also say the opposite. We are stronger with one another! When I stay connected to the body, then other members of the body are blessed. That's the beauty of the body — when we are connected, we are a blessing to everyone with whom we are connected!

My son had his first game last week. He is coming into his own as a strong player! As a proud father, I thought he would be made a starter. All week, he was with the first defense and was named a captain for the first game. That said, he only got three plays. In the first play, he got the ball but didn't make a tackle. On the next play, he made a tackle. Then, in the next play, they went on a two-count, and he was called for an offsides. After which, they pulled him out of the game. For whatever reason, he didn't play much more after that. I'm not going to lie - I was not pleased. I wanted them to put my boy back in, but they didn't. On my son's team, we have a lot of young ballers. And when I looked down at the sideline, I promise you my son celebrated way more for his teammates than for himself.

I learned a lot from my son that day.

That's the beauty of a team. My son had accepted that when his teammates succeed, he also succeeds. How different would your team, job, or family be if you had that attitude? In life, we might not know who will score next, but I hope we can celebrate more for our brothers and sisters than we do for ourselves. The more my son works to benefit others, the more he benefits. Based on your actions, which is true for you? Do you believe that we can accomplish more together or you can accomplish more on your own?

3. The Belief in the Brotherhood

25 that there may be no division in the body, but that the members may have the same care for one another.

There are no insignificant members of the body.
That's it.
That's the lesson.

You might not be a former or current football player or even a coach, but we should be able to accept that all 11 players on the field are equally important. Maybe the QB or the RB might have more fans in the stands wearing a jersey, but they wouldn't be successful without the offensive life protecting them and opening up holes. If we can understand that principle on the football field, should we not understand it in life? On the field of play, we are not competing against one another but we are there to support one another. I know you believe in yourself, but I want to give you homework.

Before the next kickoff, before the next meeting, or before the next family gathering, I want you to find one person and encourage them. Lift them up. Celebrate them. Let them know how much they matter and mean to you. I want you to tell them how much you love them and how thankful you are to be their teammate, coworker, or family member. A little gratitude goes a long way. And when we're together, we can go further than we'd ever imagine possible.

DEVOTIONAL
CHARLOTTE, NC
SATURDAY, SEPTEMBER 4, 2021

MINDSET: WE ARE BETTER TOGETHER

1. THE BLESSING OF A BROTHERHOOD
- When God gives us a gift, that gift won't always look like what we expect.
- Our commitment to one another is our response to God's commitment to us.
- To be baptized by the Spirit means that we belong to Christ's body. To be filled with the Spirit means that our bodies belong to Christ.
- What you do must be separated from who you are.

2. THE BEAUTY OF A BROTHERHOOD
- We must remember that we are a part of something that is much bigger than one person.
- Based upon your actions, which mindset do you possess; one that says *"I can accomplish more with my brothers"* or, one that says *"I can accomplish more on my own"*.
- We must stay connected for the benefit of others and for the benefit of ourselves.

3. THE BELIEF OF A BROTHERHOOD
- There are no insignificant brothers!
- Diversity leads to disunity when brothers have an unhealthy competition with one another, but diversity leads to unity when the brothers commit to one another.
- Do you believe in your brothers? Or do you simply believe in yourself?

1 Corinthians 12

¹² For just as the body is one and has many members, and all the members of the body, though many, are one body, so it is with Christ. ⋯⋯ ¹⁴ For the body does not consist of one member but of many. ¹⁵ If the foot should say, "Because I am not a hand, I do not belong to the body," that would not make it any less a part of the body. ¹⁶ And if the ear should say, "Because I am not an eye, I do not belong to the body," that would not make it any less a part of the body. ¹⁷ If the whole body were an eye, where would be the sense of hearing? If the whole body were an ear, where would be the sense of smell? ¹⁸ But as it is, God arranged the members in the body, each one of them, as he chose. ¹⁹ If all were a single member, where would the body be? ²⁰ As it is, there are many parts, yet one body. ²¹ The eye cannot say to the hand, "I have no need of you," nor again the head to the feet, "I have no need of you." ²² On the contrary, the parts of the body that seem to be weaker are indispensable, ²³ and on those parts of the body that we think less honorable we bestow the greater honor, and our unpresentable parts are treated with greater modesty, ²⁴ which our more presentable parts do not require. But God has so composed the body, giving greater honor to the part that lacked it, ²⁵ that there may be no division in the body, but that the members may have the same care for one another.

BANK OF AMERICA STADIUM

Rk	Date	Opponent	Result	Passing					Rushing				Total Offense			First Downs				Penalties		Turnovers		
				Cmp	Att	Pct	Yds	TD	Att	Yds	Avg	TD	Plays	Yds	Avg	Pass	Rush	Pen	Tot	No.	Yds	Fum	Int	Tot
1	9/4/21	N. Clemson	W (10-3)	22	30	73.3	135	0	31	121	3.9	0	61	256	4.2	7	6	2	15	10	94	1	1	2

W 10-3
GAME TIME: 7:30 P.M. EST
GAME ATTENDANCE: 74,187

CHAPTER 2
KNOWING WHY

ATHENS, GA
SEPTEMBER 11, 2021

15 For this reason, because I have heard of your faith in the Lord Jesus and your love toward all the saints, 16 I do not cease to give thanks for you, remembering you in my prayers, 17 that the God of our Lord Jesus Christ, the Father of glory, may give you the Spirit of wisdom and of revelation in the knowledge of him, 18 having the eyes of your hearts enlightened, that you may know what is the hope to which he has called you, what are the riches of his glorious inheritance in the saints, 19 and what is the immeasurable greatness of his power toward us who believe.
Ephesians 1:15-19

Have you heard of William Randolph Hearst? A wildly successful American businessman and newspaper publisher, Hearst is mainly known for developing the nation's largest newspaper chain and media company Hearst Communications. While Hearst was successful in the newspaper business, his greatest passion was collecting art from around the world. One day, Mr. Hearst discovered a description of a valuable piece of art that intrigued him. The more he read about it, the more he felt convinced that he had to own it. He went about searching for it himself but was unsuccessful at locating the elusive piece of art. Later, he enlisted the help of an art broker to help him in his pursuit. Finally, after months of searching, the broker reported that he had found the item.

When the broker called Mr. Hearst, he told him that he would be shocked about the discovery. What was shocking about the broker's discovery was not the cost to acquire the item or even its condition. The most shocking detail about the discovery was the location of the item. The piece of art that Mr. Hearst had so desperately desired was actually in his personal warehouse! Hearst had been searching frantically for something he already possessed. He was looking on the outside for something that he already possessed on the inside. Had he simply read the catalog of his treasures, he would have saved himself a great deal of time, money, and trouble.

When we consider the story of Mr. Hearst, and how he failed to recognize what he already possessed on the inside, I am reminded of the importance of knowing our why. Our why should not be driven by something on the outside; our why must come from something on the inside. When we really take the time to identify our why, we should be able to see how the tests, temptations, and trials of life can easily cause us to forget or lose sight of our why. That's why I'm thankful for the opportunity to serve as a minister because I am here to help you know your why, but I'm also here to help you see how God influences our why.

I love our passage today because it is written so that we know why and how we live for God's glory. In the book of Ephesians, the Apostle Paul is writing to remind the church of what we already possess in Christ! Paul wants us to know something. He wants us to know why God loves us, and he wants us to know why God is calling us! Paul is saying, "Let me tell you about the blessings and benefits we have in Jesus." Specifically, the apostle Paul is led to write the letter out of the simple desire for the people of God to know what they have been given by the grace of God through Christ Jesus.

Paul doesn't waste time; he jumps right into the letter and begins to share what the Lord Has given us. In verse 4, Paul reminds us that God has chosen us (v. 4). God tells us that we are chosen. Thereby meaning God initiated the relationship, not us. In verse 5, he reminds us that God has adopted us (v. 5). We are now a part of the family of God. Yes, we all have a biological family, but Paul is teaching us that we also have a spiritual family. When Christ sacrificed his life on the cross, that sacrifice allowed us to be a part of a new family. This means that the color that has to be at the forefront of our minds, cannot be the color of our skin or even the social class in which we operate. The color that matters most is the shed blood of Calvary that covers our life. One of the reasons why I love being a minister of the Lord is the encouragement I receive from my diverse community of believers. To take it a step further, it's not simply that the community is diverse, but it's that this is precisely what God desires for everyone to experience.

Picture it this way. There will likely not be a more unified time during the week than when folks are together rooting for their team inside of the stadium. Black folks, white folks, Latinos, and Asians - everyone will be together in one spirit and in one purpose. In our passage today, Paul reminds us that we were chosen and adopted by God, but we were also accepted into God's family. In verse 6, Paul reminds us that Jesus accepted us. It is a reminder that God's acceptance of us is not based upon anything we have done. Since God knows the end from the beginning and the beginning from the end, we must understand that God chose to accept us knowing that we would make mistakes. God accepted you, knowing that you would mess up. He knew that you would have fears and doubts and struggles. When God accepts us, we must understand that we are accepted without having to perform for it.

Sometimes, you'll see or hear sermons preached where it's an obvious attempt to guilt people into performing for God. We want to guilt people into going to church more, serving more, giving more — more, more, more, more! As if doing more of anything would actually impress God. I'm guilty of it myself. I do it too. Anytime I get to this point, I try to remind myself of a very sobering thought. God is not like me. God is not in heaven waiting for us to impress Him. He's waiting for us to trust Him!

God has not only accepted us, but he has also redeemed and forgiven us as we see from verse 7. This means that Christ paid the ultimate penalty, and the payment has been made in full. Just in verse 10, Paul tells us that God has chosen us, adopted us, accepted us, redeemed us, and forgiven us. And in verse 13, Paul tells us that God has sealed us. This speaks to the finality of the act. What God has done, cannot be lost.

When we hear about all that God has done, we certainly should be excited, but we should also ask a significant question — Do I know what God has provided? Also, am I taking advantage of what God has provided? Not too long ago at all, we were in the middle of a global pandemic. The government made a decision to give out stimulus checks as so many people found themselves experiencing financial difficulties. I recently came across an article that mentioned how many people, over 1.2 million Americans, failed to claim their stimulus check. That translates to roughly over 2 billion in unclaimed stimulus money. The government is trying its best to let people know that this money is available, but it's not being claimed.

In our text, Paul is praying that we know something about God. Paul knew that for the people to receive the truth, God would have to reveal the truth. So, in verse 15, Paul begins to pray. Paul recognized that he did not possess the ability to change people, but God could. God could speak to the hearts of people so that we know and believe but also so that we experience God's best! First, Paul prays that we know God's calling!

1. Knowing God's Calling

18 having the eyes of your hearts enlightened, that you may know what is the hope to which he has called you, what are the riches of his glorious inheritance in the saints,

Our hope impacts how we live. If you are looking for a definition of hope please know that hope is more than wishful thinking. Hope is more than positive thinking. Hope is a confident expectation. Go back with me to when you were getting recruited to go to college, or the military, or a job. What was your hope? What was your confident expectation? You had a confident expectation to get stronger. You had a confident expectation that you would be successful. It wasn't just wishful thinking. It was a confident expectation. Think about the last big game you played in, or the last big test you had to take. Were you looking for a warm fuzzy feeling? No. What you needed and desired was confidence. Hope is important because hope impacts what we believe and how we live. Now if we can understand that athletically, academically, or professionally, how much more should we be able to understand that spiritually?

As believers, we must consider our calling. What has Christ called you to do? I know what you're thinking — right now, you're reading this thinking, is T. Settles trying to make me a preacher? Let me clearly say that we are called to be like Christ. How did Christ live? He walked in humility. He was focused on serving others. He spoke truth in love with conviction and with compassion. Christ cared for people. He showed his commitment to others, by his willingness to lay down his life so that we could enjoy eternal life! Jesus made disciples. He invested in others who would, in turn, invest in others. He knew he wouldn't always be here physically, so He wanted to pour into others who would pour into others when He was gone.

Let me pause and ask you a question....is that an expectation that you have for yourself?

{Insert Your Name}, am I living in a way where I'd have a confident expectation that my life reflects Christ's? Who am I pouring into today? Will it be someone who will pour into someone else once I'm gone?

Imagine you're on a team, and your eligibility is almost up. When you're gone, who will stand in your place to pour into others? We are called to do this because this is what Christ did. Some might be thinking, that's too much, bro. That's not really for me.

Consider the story of the African missionary who talks about taking the gospel to a new tribe in the northern part of the continent. To get to the unreached village, he had to go past where most common people would go. Knowing that he needed some help, the missionary appealed to a local chief to get a guide. The missionary asked if there was anyone in the village who would serve as a guide and take him to the distant northern tribe. The chief summoned a man — tall, battle-scarred, carrying a large. The missionary and the man agreed to a price and the next morning, the missionary set out through the bush following his new guide. The way became increasingly rough, and the path all but disappeared. There was an occasional mark cut on a tree or a freshly cut narrow path here and there, but overall, it was a maze-like jungle. After hiking for several hours, the missionary called out to the man and asked him to stop for a break.

Though the missionary was tired and exhausted, he was also anxious about his progress. In his heart, he was very intimidated by the guide, but he couldn't help but wonder if the man was leading him the right way. Though very apprehensive, his curiosity got the best of him, and the missionary mustered up enough courage to ask the guide.

"Are you truly sure you know the way?"

The guide was very offended by the question and took a moment just to stare at the man.

After taking a breath, he responded, "Sir, do you see this ax in my hand? Do you see these scars on my body? With this ax, I blazed a trail to the village where we met. Where you are trying to go is where I came from. You asked me if I knew the way.

Before I came, there was no way. Sir, I am the way."

That's Jesus. Jesus came to show us the way. And now Jesus is calling us to show others the way. Not in a way where we are unloving and adversarial, but in a way that is humble, loving, and consistent.

2. Knowing God's Care

18 having the eyes of your hearts enlightened, that you may know what is the hope to which he has called you, what are the riches of his glorious inheritance in the saints,

Paul prays first that we might know the hope of God's calling, but secondly, he prays that we accept how valuable we are to God. Because of past sins and failures, many of us have bought the lie that God is angry and disgusted with us. We think that God looks down on us in perpetual judgment and wishes we could get it together. We think that God is in heaven just waiting to zap us. We think God is in heaven setting up traps for us to fail. Nothing could be further from the truth. The reality is that when we place our trust in Christ, God looks at us and sees sons and daughters. He sees someone who has been redeemed and forgiven. He sees someone that is created in His likeness and image. He sees someone with purpose. He sees someone who is a part of His plan and able to fulfill His purpose.

How different would our lives be if we saw ourselves how God sees us? How different would our lives be if we saw others how God sees them? Think for a second. Let's say you hit the lottery. What would be something that you would automatically possess? Take some time and identify it. Could it be a house? Could it be a car? Perhaps it would be some jewelry or an expensive piece of art? If you hit the lottery, what would be the most valuable thing you possess?

OK, you thought of it, right?

Now that you have identified it, let me ask a follow-up question. How do you want people to treat it? Your prized possession – the house, the car, the jewelry, or the painting – if someone had to take care of it for you – how would you want them to handle your most prized possession?

I don't know if you realize this, but you are God's most prized possession. God's most prized possession will never be something material or temporal like a house, car, or clothes. God's most prized possession is His people, which means that we are valuable to God. And just like we have an expectation for people to take care of our most prized possession, God has an expectation that we care for His most prized possession — other people.

3. Knowing God's Commitment

19 and what is the immeasurable greatness of his power toward us who believe, according to the working of his great might 20 that he worked in Christ when he raised him from the dead and seated him at his right hand in the heavenly places, 21 far above all rule and authority and power and dominion, and above every name that is named, not only in this age but also in the one to come. 22 And he put all things under his feet and gave him as head over all things to the church, 23 which is his body, the fullness of him who fills all in all.

In the text, we clearly see that God is so committed to us that the same power that was at work in the life of Christ, is at work in our lives also! Just for a second, think about the life of Christ. Think about how many people counted him out. Think about how the text reminds us that Jesus is seated above all, which communicates his ultimate power and authority. Here is the truth – it doesn't matter how bad life gets. It doesn't matter who might come against you in life. Jesus has higher authority which means whatever or whoever you are dealing with doesn't have the final say! Amen, somebody?

We need to understand that authority is important because authority reveals the right to rule. In a football game, the referees are not the biggest, strongest, or fastest people on the field. But when they throw the yellow flag, the game must stop because of their authority. The players are far more powerful than the referees, but they have a different level of authority. As a believer, you have even been given spiritual authority. Yes, Satan certainly comes at you with a powerful attack. But that power is devoid of divine authority. Satan's attack is real. He would like you to think that life will never get better; that you will always be alone; that God has forgotten about you. He wants you to think that everyone is against you. That the sickness has no cure.

We can rest in the reality that God's power is always greater than our problems. In the Bible, most people counted David out, but with God's power, he was to experience victory. In the Bible, people counted Daniel out, but with God's power, he was able to experience victory. The people counted Nehemiah out, but with God's power, he was able to experience victory. In life, people will try to count you out, but that's okay. Because when we are willing to do God's will, we can have access to God's power and we too can experience victory!

GAME TWO
DEVOTIONAL CARD

DEVOTIONAL
ATHENS, GA
SATURDAY, SEPTEMBER 11, 2021

KNOWING WHY

1. KNOWING GOD'S CALLING
- God has called us 'to something' and 'for something'. We are called to be like Christ.
- While we all have a biological family, God has invited us to be adopted into a spiritual family for eternity.
- A man who does not know his high calling (Phil. 3:14), holy calling (2 Tim. 1:9), and heavenly calling (Heb. 3:1) will never be able to walk worthy of that calling.

2. KNOWING GOD'S CARE
- Paul is praying that the people know how valuable they are to Christ.
- Just as a man's wealth brings glory to his name, so God will get glory from us because of what He has invested in us.
- God deals with us based on our future in heaven, not our past mistakes on earth.

3. KNOWING GOD'S COMMITMENT
- God's people do not fight for victory, but from victory!
- The greatest power shortage today is not in our generators or our gas tanks. It is in our personal lives.

Ephesians 1

15 For this reason, because I have heard of your faith in the Lord Jesus and your love toward all the saints, 16 I do not cease to give thanks for you, remembering you in my prayers, 17 that the God of our Lord Jesus Christ, the Father of glory, may give you the Spirit of wisdom and of revelation in the knowledge of him, 18 having the eyes of your hearts enlightened, that you may know what is the hope to which he has called you, what are the riches of his glorious inheritance in the saints, 19 and what is the immeasurable greatness of his power toward us who believe!

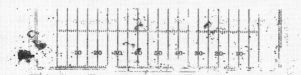

W 56-7
GAME TIME: 3:30 P.M. EST
GAME ATTENDANCE: 92,746

Rk	Date	Opponent	Result	Passing					Rushing				Total Offense			First Downs				Penalties		Turnovers		
				Cmp	Att	Pct	Yds	TD	Att	Yds	Avg	TD	Plays	Yds	Avg	Pass	Rush	Pen	Tot	No.	Yds	Fum	Int	Tot
2	9/11/21	Alabama-Birmingham	W (56-7)	14	22	63.6	376	6	38	163	4.3	1	60	539	9	10	11	2	23	4	47	0	1	1

SANFORD STADIUM

CHAPTER 3
TOUGHNESS

ATHENS, GA
SEPTEMBER 18, 2021

11 And next to him was Shammah, the son of Agee the Hararite. The Philistines gathered together at Lehi, where there was a plot of ground full of lentils, and the men fled from the Philistines. 12 But he took his stand in the midst of the plot and defended it and struck down the Philistines, and the Lord worked a great victory.
2 Samuel 23:11-12

Yesterday, we had the privilege of hearing from the Five Pioneers —or the first Black players to sign with and ultimately play varsity football for the Bulldogs. Over 50 years ago, 5 African-American players integrated the UGA team. The names, Richard Appleby, Chuck Kinnebrew, Horace King, Clarence Pope, and Larry West, made history as the first African-American scholarship football players at the University of Georgia. They did something that had never been done before. And 50 years later, what they accomplished is still being talked about today. Just think for a second, what are you doing right now that will matter in 50 years? What are you doing this year that will mean anything in the 2070s?

I know everyone reading this devotional hasn't had the privilege of hearing their story, so let me encourage you to take some time out to research those brothers. But if you take the time to gain more information about the First Five, I firmly believe you will leave convinced that their journey was anything but easy. It certainly would have been easier for them to attend an HBCU. They could have gone to a Morehouse. They could have gone to a South Carolina State. They could have gone to Tennessee State or Grambling. We have to remember that in those days, HBCUs were producing high-caliber NFL players just like the big schools. Players like Walter Payton, Ed "Too Tall" Jones, Shannon Sharp, Michael Strahan, Steve "Air" McNair, and

T. Settles all went to an HBCU. For the Five Pioneers, it would have been so much easier to attend an HBCU, but they wanted to be at UGA.

I bring them up because they will be honored at the game today, but I also want to bring them up because of what they shared yesterday. When they shared their story with the team, they certainly spoke about playing for Coach Dooly, getting to play in the Sanford stadium, and having success on the field. But the thing that I remember most distinctly from their talk was that they wanted to put more pressure on themselves than anyone else. They felt responsible for one another, and they agreed to be harder on themselves than the coaches or other players. They understood the responsibility that was before them. They understood that the entire campus was watching them. Fans, coaches, teammates, professors, and other students were all seeing how they were going to do. They realized that this opportunity was too important to not give it their very best. So, for this reason, they agreed that they would be tougher on each other than anyone else could be on them. Tougher than the coaches. Tougher than other teammates. Tougher than professors. The standard they held for themselves was greater than anyone else could put on them. I love their example because they challenge us - that in life, nothing worthwhile will ever be easy. We live in a day and time where most players and most men in general are looking for the easy way out. In our culture today, we rarely want to take the road less traveled. We prefer the easiest route possible, but these men decided to do things the hard way. And because of their toughness, we are still talking about what they accomplished today.

Dream with me for a second. In your life personally and on our team publicly, what could be accomplished if we embraced toughness? What if on the team or in the marriage or in the company, a group of people got together and made the decision to increase the pressure? I get excited thinking about what could happen 50 years from now if we embraced the attitude that I want to be tougher on my brothers or sisters than the coaches. I want to be tougher on my brothers and sisters than the folks in our academic support department. I want to be tougher because I want what we do today to matter in the next 50 years. I want to fully grasp the idea that what I do each and every day is so important that I won't take the easy way out. I won't run to what is comfortable. I won't run to what is easy, but I want to run to what is hard. Because what I'm doing is important. As I think about the First Five of UGA as well as the man mentioned in our text today, I'm encouraged because I see what God did in their lives, and I catch a glimpse of what God can do in my life.

Let me clear something up. Sometimes in reading the Bible, we can begin to think, I need to be more like the characters in the text. When I read about David it's easy to think that I need to be more like him. He was the underdog amid a big fight, and when I face a huge challenge, I need to summon the strength of my inner David and slay the Goliaths in my life. Or perhaps I need to be more like Peter? I mean, Peter was faithful, and he walked on water during a tumultuous storm. So, when I am facing life's challenges, I need to have that kind of big faith so I, too, can walk on water, right? We do that with David and Moses and Joshua and Nehemiah. It's pretty common behavior. However, if you have ever approached the Bible that way, I want to offer you an alternative. When we read the Bible, we must always remember that these characters in scripture are not models for morality, but rather mirrors for identity. When we read passages in the scriptures, we should never conclude that we need to be more like anybody *but* Jesus. Reading this, you might be thinking, "Ok, T. Sett, then how am I to read the Bible then?"

I'm so glad you asked!

As we read the Bible, we are called to reflect on the faithfulness of God in the lives of other people. And that should remind us that since God has been faithful in the past, we can trust that God will be faithful in the present. That is how we should approach 2 Samuel 23. In the passage, there is a long list of names. Specifically, there is a long list of men who went into battle and came out with the victory. Today, I want to focus on a man by the name of Shammah. We don't know much about the man, but earlier in the text, he is referred to as one of David's Mighty Men. His life is a reminder that we don't have to have our name called often to be mighty, but we must be ready.

When I moved to Athens in 2007, I didn't serve the football team. I was primarily with the basketball team. In my first year, I got close to a player by the name of Sundiata Gaines. Sundiata was from

Brooklyn, and he had a dream of making it to the NBA. Leaving Athens, he went undrafted, and he started his first couple of seasons in the NBA G League (then known as the D League). During the 2010 season, the Utah Jazz had some injuries, so they signed him on a 10-day contract. They really didn't have a long-term plan for him. They were just waiting on the other guys to get back healthy and needed to hold water with fresh bodies. His name wasn't called much, but on January 25th, he hit a game-winner at the buzzer to beat the Cavs. What I love about him and his story is that he chased his dream. It didn't happen how he had planned it. It was far from a perfect or ideal scenario. But he was ready when his name was called. That is also true of Shammah. We must understand that Shammah was at home. He was responsible for protecting his land. He was responsible for protecting his home turf, and even though the passage does not give us many details, three things stick out:

1. Toughness requires the conviction to take a stand.

Verse 11 says again, *"The Philistines gathered together at Lehi, where there was a plot of ground full of lentils, and the men fled from the Philistines. 12 But he took his stand in the midst of the plot and defended it*

While other men ran away, this man was willing to take a stand. When other men neglected their responsibility, this man took advantage of the opportunity, and he defended the land that he had been given. This past April marked the 53rd anniversary of the assassination of Rev. Dr. Martin Luther King Jr. When we consider the life of Dr. King, we must not focus on how he died but, more importantly, on how he lived. Don't believe the lie that he was weak or that his strategy of nonviolent resistance was soft. He was tough. He didn't run away from things that were hard. He lived his life defending the freedoms that we had been given by God and the Constitution. Dr. King is remembered for saying, "If a man has not found something worth dying for, he is not fit to live." It's 53 years after he died, but we celebrate the life he lived! He lived taking a stand for what is important! Can you remember a time in your life when you decided to take a stand? Can you remember a time in your life when you decided to defend something that you have been given? Not just for you. Not just for your stock to rise. Not just to increase your stats or your reputation? Have you ever truly taken a stand to be a blessing to other people?

In our text, Shammah taking a stand required him to see more than just a field of lentils. A lentil is just some peas. The passage tells us that when he saw the field of peas he decided to take a stand. My brothers and sisters, I want you to know that he was taking a stand for more than just peas. In their culture, people would have to grow their food, and usually, when nations were at war, they would burn fields of food to starve the people. When Shammah saw the lentils, he saw the lives that would be impacted. I want you to catch the details here. His decision to take a stand was not something that would have only impacted him. Every one of those lentils or peas was a picture of a life that would be impacted. To allow the lentils to be destroyed would be the equivalent of the lives of the people being destroyed. So, rather than allowing that to happen, he decided to defend the land, and he made the decision to take a stand.

When we think about that lentil field, we should be reminded of the blessings that God has placed in our lives. And here is the thing about a blessing. God does not simply want to bless you, but God does want to make you a blessing. Every gift that God has entrusted to us should be viewed the same way as Shammah viewed that lentil field. If you are fortunate enough to get a scholarship, that is just like that lentil field. If you have a family, that is just like that lentil field. If you have a career, that is just like that lentil field. This means that you have to defend it, and you need to take a stand to protect it. After the game is over and you are hanging out with your friends, the decisions that you make will either bless your lentil field or burden it. What you do after work will either bless your lentil field or burden it. What you do when no one is looking will either bless your lentil field or burden it. What you decide to put in your body. Who you decide to hang with. What things you decide to skip or attend — all those things are blessings or burdens to life's lentil field.

We must remember that taking a stand is not simply reserved for the "field," but for every day in every way for Christ. That means we are going to protect the things that God says are important.

Do you remember in the fall of 2021 when the rapper Lil Baby bought a fake watch for $400,000? He thought that he was buying a real Patek Philippe, but it turned out to be a Fugazi.

Someone got him to believe that it was important and valuable when in reality, it was fake. I believe the same exact thing happens with Satan in our lives. Satan is trying to scam us. Satan is trying to get us to place value on something that God says is not valuable. Satan is trying to get you to throw away your hard work on things that are worthless. Taking a stand requires toughness because it is hard to not be confused by what is real vs what is fake. Taking a stand is hard because it requires us to reject Satan's bait.

2. Toughness Requires the Courage to Get into a Fight.

12 But he took his stand in the midst of the plot and defended it and struck down the Philistines,

Now it is one thing to take a stand, but it is another thing to get in a fight. When Shammah saw the lentil field, he didn't simply see peas. He saw all the people who would be impacted. It's not just that, though. He also saw all the hard work that went into getting the crops ready. That's why he was willing to fight. He had worked too hard to run away from a "good" fight. Is that not true today? Have we not put in too much work not to fight? Have we not invested too much time and energy to waste it? In the text, Shammah valued feeding his family more than he feared the fight. When we think about a fight we must remember that the "fight" is not just for a victory in a game but for a victorious life. Do you guys know that God doesn't simply want you to be victorious in a football game, but God wants you to be victorious in life. The only way to achieve that is to get into a good fight.

This might shock some of y'all, but I wasn't the greatest athlete in high school. I have to say that because you better figure out how to add value. Some ball out on Saturday. Some help the team get a good look in practice. And other guys help the team's GPA. In college, I would give a decent look, but the most value I added was the team GPA. School was something that came easily to me, which meant I had to put more work into the areas in which I struggled. A good fight isn't simply about the areas that come easy. It's about the areas where you struggle.

The good fights include pursuing purity.

The good fights include walking in humility.

The good fights include getting a degree.

The good fights include serving your spouse.

The good fights include investing in your children.

The good fights include being a light to your community!

All of these things can happen, if and only if, you are willing to get into the good fights of life!

3. Toughness Requires the Commitment to Give God All the Praise.

... and the Lord worked a great victory.

Since God provides the will to stand, the strength to fight, and the skill to win, then God desires all the praise. We know that God desires all the praise, but the truth is God deserves all the praise. There is something within us that wants to take the credit for what we accomplish.

Many of us know the name Alexander Graham Bell because he is often referred to as the inventor of the telephone. Long before there was an iPhone or an android, Bell was awarded the first patent for the telephone. While he gets the credit, that is not the true story. Before Bell applied for his patent, a man by the name of Anthony Meucci applied for a telephone patent as well. However, since he was a poor immigrant, he did not have the money to file the patent, and in time his application expired. At this point, Bell applied for his patent, and the rest is history. We don't want to admit it, but many times we are far more like Bell in life than Meucci. We want to take the credit, not just from our teammates, coaches, coworkers, or spouses but also from the Lord!

In life, it's easy to point to me. It's easy to pat ourselves on the back. I pray that we are tough enough to fight, but humble enough to give God all the credit.

DEVOTIONAL
ATHENS, GA
SATURDAY, SEPTEMBER 18, 2021

DNA: TOUGHNESS

1. TOUGHNESS REQUIRES THE CONVICTION TO TAKE A STAND.
- Our convictions should be connected to our "why"
- Do you possess the conviction to take a stand?
- Taking a stand required Shammah to see more than just a field of lentils. Taking a stand is not simply reserved for the "field," but every day, in every way, for Christ.

2. TOUGHNESS REQUIRES THE COURAGE TO GET IN THE FIGHT.
- Shammah worked too hard to run away from a "good" fight.
- Shammah valued feeding his family more than he feared the fight.
- We must remember that God doesn't simply want you to be victorious in a game but God wants you to be victorious in life.

3. TOUGHNESS REQUIRES THE COMMITMENT TO GIVE GOD ALL THE PRAISE.
- Since God provides the will to stand, the strength to fight, and the skill to win – God desires all the praise.
- The "praise" is not simply offered when we get what we want, but when we recognize what God has offered us through Christ.

2 Samuel 23

11 And next to him was Shammah, the son of Agee the Hararite. The Philistines gathered together at Lehi, where there was a plot of ground full of lentils; and the men fled from the Philistines. 12 But he took his stand in the midst of the plot and defended it and struck down the Philistines, and the Lord worked a great victory.

Rk	Date	Opponent	Result	Cmp	Att	Pct	Yds	TD	Att	Yds	Avg	TD	Plays	Yds	Avg	Rush	Pass	Pen	Tot	No.	Yds	Fum	Int	Tot
				Passing					Rushing				Total Offense			First Downs				Penalties		Turnovers		
3	9/18/21	South Carolina	W (40-13)	24	35	68.6	307	3	31	184	5.9	2	66	491	7.4	16	8	2	26	7	52	1	2	3

SANFORD STADIUM

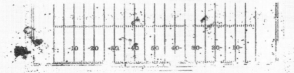

W 40-13
GAME TIME: 7:00 P.M. EST
GAME ATTENDANCE: 92,746

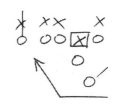

CHAPTER 4

COMPOSURE

NASHVILLE, TN
SEPTEMBER 25, 2021

1 The Lord is my shepherd; I shall not want. 2 He makes me lie down in green pastures. He leads me beside still waters. 3 He restores my soul.
He leads me in paths of righteousness for his name's sake. 4 Even though I walk through the valley of the shadow of death, I will fear no evil, for you are with me; your rod and your staff, they comfort me. 5 You prepare a table before me in the presence of my enemies; you anoint my head with oil; my cup overflows. 6 Surely goodness and mercy shall follow me all the days of my life, and I shall dwell in the house of the Lord forever.
Psalm 23:1-6

Major League Baseball has been played in America since 1875. But on September 14, 1990, something happened that has never happened before and has never happened since. Ken Griffey, Sr. who had been a key member of the World Series Champion Cincinnati Reds was now at the tail-end of his career. His son Ken Griffey, Jr. was just starting his major league career. On that day, in the first inning of a game against the Angels, Griffey, Sr. hit a home run to center field. His son then followed him to the plate and hit another home run to almost exactly the same spot. It was the only time a father and son have hit back-to-back home runs in professional baseball history. If you were to speak with Griffey, Sr. and Griffey, Jr., they would quickly tell you what took place on that field was simply an overflow of what had been taking place at home. As a father, Ken Griffey, Sr. had not simply told his son the way, he had shown him the way also. His leadership in public was preceded by his leadership in private. Because the son was prepared for what was to come, the son had composure. When I think about that story it underscores for me the value of composure. When we display composure, we have the opportunity to show others the

way. It has been said that the best leaders know the way, go the way, and show the way (John Maxwell).
And that is what we want to see on this team, in our families, and our community.

As believers, we must remember that God is calling us to know the way, and He is calling us to show the way. When I think about knowing the way, going the way, and showing the way, I am reminded of the 23rd Psalm.

Now we know that the author of the Psalm is David and as we read the text, I believe it is clear that David is trying to communicate that God is faithful. Hear me: David has composure because his heart was surrendered to the Lord. David was humble enough to ask the Lord to search his heart so that he would be made aware of any unsurrendered area. I want you to hear my heart on this one. There is not one area in your life where you can't trust God. And since David knew that he could trust God, he models what that looks like and shows us how we can trust God also. As a minister, I recognize that we are all in different places in our lives spiritually. I have the sneaky suspicion that there might be someone reading this devotional that is wondering if they are really able to trust God.

Can you really trust God in every area of your life?
Can you really trust God with football?
Can you really trust God with your career? Or with your health?
Or with your family?

I am here to tell you that there is not one area of your life where you can't trust Him. Let me take it a step further and say if there were an area of your life where God could not be trusted, then God would not be God. That is why we have composure because God is in control. Since God is God and is in full control, we can not only trust Him, but we can also help others trust him as well. That's true on your team, on your job, or in your family! We can help the people that God has planted in our lives to know the way, go the way, and show the way.

First, let's consider how David encourages us to know the way.

1. David Encourages Us to Know the Way.

1 The Lord is my shepherd

David begins by simply saying the Lord is my shepherd. A shepherd is a leader, and David declares that he is willing to follow. When David says the Lord is my shepherd, he is communicating that the Lord is my leader, and I choose to follow God. So many times, we want others to commit to following us, but we won't make the commitment to follow God first. Think for a second. Those of you who desire for people to follow you, who are they ultimately following? Are they following you as you follow Christ? Or are they following you as you follow your own dreams, goals, and desires? Are you a selfish leader not concerned about the well-being of the people following you or are you a sacrificial leader concerned about the success and growth of those who are following after you?

Here is the truth: following someone is a decision. Following is a choice. I have read this psalm so many times, but as I looked at it fresh this week, I was reminded that we have a decision to make. The Lord being our shepherd doesn't happen by accident. The Lord being my leader doesn't happen by coincidence, but the Lord being my leader requires commitment. It requires that we do more than honor the Lord with our lips. It requires that we honor the Lord with our lives. The same is true with our team or with our families. Being a great team or teammate doesn't happen by accident. It requires a huge commitment. The things you say are important. What comes out of your lips is important. But what is more important is what comes out of your life!

As humans, we can chase a lot of things. We can chase money. We can chase women. We can chase influence. We can chase possessions. We can chase the approval of people. We can chase a lot of things, but in the Psalm, David is encouraging us to give our lives to chasing God. When I do marriage counseling, I often ask the question, "What is the greatest gift that you will give to your spouse?" Some of the answers I receive from folks are communication. Honesty. Fidelity. Integrity. But I believe that the greatest gift you will give to your spouse is the commitment to follow Christ. Likewise, the greatest gift that we can give to our children is the commitment to follow Christ. Because even when I don't feel like it, commitment causes me to put others before myself, and it gives the other person a model to follow. The decision to make the Lord your leader means that we want God to be pleased with every area of our lives.

What is the greatest gift that we give to our team? Is it a touchdown? Is it making a great play? Is it getting to a great bowl game? What about your family? What is the greatest gift that you give to your family? Is it just going to college? Is it just making some money? Is it just being able to provide nice possessions? I want to submit to you that the greatest gift that we give to our team, our families, or our community is our commitment to Christ.

The greatest gift that we will give our team is a model to follow. A model for how to practice. A model for how to study. A model for how to take care of things off the field. A model for how to deal with adversity. A model to follow when things are not easy and or going great. And if you are a believer, then we have so much more we can give. If you have placed your trust in Christ, then you have the responsibility to provide a model for prayer. A model for patience. A model for perseverance. A model for living out your purpose.

Brothers and sisters, that is what God is calling us to do. God desires that we faithfully follow Christ and that we make the Lord our leader. Sometimes we make excuses about what we cannot do. Maybe you won't start tomorrow. Maybe you won't run the football tomorrow. Maybe you won't catch a pass. Maybe you won't sign a huge NIL deal. But we can operate in such a way that those around us will have a model to follow. Can you say that right now as you look at your life, is your life a model for others to follow? When you're not playing as much as you want, or when you aren't having a ton of success - do you still faithfully follow Christ? What about what you're doing off the field? What do you do in your marriage? What do you do with your finances? Will you allow Christ to lead and guide you?

Here is the truth. When the Lord is leading, we will be humble. When the Lord is leading, we will be strong. When the Lord is leading, we will have composure. When the Lord is leading, I will put others before myself because when God leads us, our lives are not perfect, but they are certainly different.

David also says, "The Lord is my shepherd." The Lord *"is"*, notice that David uses the present tense in the Psalm. He doesn't say: "was" or "will be," he says He is! As we focus on the present "is" we need to be careful to be where our feet are. The Lord is present tense. It's not looking back. It's not looking forward. It's being present. It's not focusing on AUB, South Carolina, or Clemson. And it's not focusing on Arkansas, Auburn, or Kentucky. It's being focused on why we are in Nashville. It's being focused on the now.

First, David encourages us to know the way, but secondly, David encourages us with what happens when we go the way.

2. David Encourages Us to Go the Way

...I shall not want.

2 He makes me lie down in green pastures. He leads me beside still waters. 3 He restores my soul. He leads me in paths of righteousness for his name's sake. 4 Even though I walk through the valley of the shadow of death, I will fear no evil, for you are with me; your rod and your staff, they comfort me.

What I love about the Psalm is the fact David takes the time to remind us about the divine benefits that come when we follow the Lord. First, David reminds us of the divine provision in the "I shall not want." David is confessing that he believes not only that

God can provide, but also that the Lord will provide for all of our needs. Then in verse 2, he speaks about divine rest. He makes me to lie down in green pastures. David says he makes me to lie down. God cares enough about me to slow me down. Anybody with children should be able to understand this analogy. You make your kids lie down not because you are upset with them, but because you know what is best for them.

You want them to lie down because if they don't lie down, they won't enter into rest. Why do coaches and support staff stay on you about going to sleep and getting rest? They do that because, like the Lord, they want you to be able to perform at your best!

Then in the next portion of verse 3, he tells us about divine peace. He leads me beside the still waters. Some might be wondering why the still waters. In the culture, people would know that all sheep would stop to drink, but if the stream were moving fast, then they would lose their footing when they got into the water. And because their wool would soak up the water, it would be impossible for them to get out of it. God puts us in a position where we can receive what we need and enjoy it.

Next, the passage mentions divine restoration. He restores my soul. Divine provision, divine peace, and divine rest will restore our souls. Then divine righteousness means when we follow him, the Shepherd gives us what we need even when we don't deserve it!

How can I have composure? I can trust that God will supply all of my needs. David encourages us to know the way. David reminds us of what will happen when we go the way. And finally, David encourages us to show the way.

3. David Encourages Us to Show the Way.

4 Even though I walk through the valley of the shadow of death, I will fear no evil; For You are with me; Your rod and Your staff, they comfort me. 5 You prepare a table before me in the presence of my enemies; You anoint my head with oil; My cup overflows

What is interesting about verses 1 through 3 is that we see the tremendous benefits that come when we go the way. But in verse 4, we must be careful in how we read the passage because on the surface it seems like the benefits have run out. In just a verse or two, we go from lying down in green pastures to being in the valley of the shadow of death. How'd we get here? Well, composure is revealed not simply when things are easy and comfortable, but perhaps most importantly, in seasons of trials and tribulations. In this section, David speaks about valleys. We must understand that this is painting a mental picture for us. A mountaintop is a place of blessing. It is usually the place where good things happen. You know you are on the mountaintop when your

family is good. You are on the mountaintop when you're getting SEC weekly honors. You are on the mountaintop when you're getting stats. On the mountaintop, everything is all good, but the reality in this life is that one can't live going from mountaintop to mountaintop. To get from one mountaintop to another, we all must go through the valley.

In our text, David is reminding us that since life can't be lived on the mountaintop, we must be prepared to go to the valley. And as we go to the valley, we show people that God is with us even there. We can be okay with the valley because the Lord is also present in the valley!

God is not just present when you get the offer or when you sign the scholarship. He's not just present when you get the job or receive a good report. God is also present when we get injured. God is present when I'm not playing as much as I want. God is present when things are hard. When the coach is riding me. When family members are sick. We know that the Lord is present in the valley because the text says, "You are with me."

There is a story about the great American preacher Dr. Donald Grey Barnhouse whose wife died at a fairly young age. The death of Dr. Barnhouse's wife left him and a six-year-old daughter in deep mourning. Barnhouse had difficulty working through his own grief, but the hardest part was attempting to comfort and explain the reality of death to his young daughter. He later recalled that all of his education and theological training left him at a loss. One day he and his little girl were standing on a busy corner at a downtown intersection waiting for a light to change. Suddenly a very large truck sped by the corner, briefly blocking out the sun and frightening the little girl. To comfort her, Dr. Barnhouse picked her up, and in a moment, filled with wisdom from God, he was able to communicate the truth about death to his daughter.

Speaking to his daughter, he said, "When you saw the truck pass, it scared you. But let me ask you, would you rather be struck by the truck or the shadow of the truck?"

She replied, "Of course, the shadow."

He went on to explain, "When your mother died, she was only hit by the shadow of Death because Jesus was hit by the truck (Death)."

In Psalms, there is a mention of death, but we are invited to show the world that we are not to fear because what we face are shadows. Shadows might scare us, but they will never be able to harm us.

The shadow of a dog can't bite.

The shadow of a sword cannot kill.

The shadow of a gun cannot shoot.

The shadow of death cannot harm God's child.

David says I will fear no evil because I will choose to focus on the shepherd rather than the shadow. When you are in the valley, will you focus on the shadow or the shepherd? David encourages us to know the way, go the way, and show the way.

Knowing the way is a privilege. We know the way when we are in the Word. Going the way is a privilege. We honor God with our lives, not just our lips. Showing the way is a privilege. We show the way when we invest in other disciples.

DEVOTIONAL
NASHVILLE, TN
SATURDAY, SEPTEMBER 25, 2021

COMPOSURE

1. DAVID ENCOURAGES US TO KNOW THE WAY
- David begins with a simple confession: "The Lord is my shepherd."
  He communicates that the Lord is his leader because he is willing to follow.
- Many times we want to lead, but are we willing to follow?

2. DAVID ENCOURAGES US TO GO THE WAY
- David continues by confessing that the "The Lord is my provider," therefore I shall not want.
- David confesses that he not only believes that God can provide, but that God will provide.
- David also confesses that the Lord will provide peace.

3. DAVID ENCOURAGES US TO SHOW THE WAY
- Composure is revealed not simply when things are easy and comfortable, but most importantly, in seasons of trials and tribulations.
- Since life can't be lived only on the mountain top, you must be prepared to go the valley. And when we're in the valley, we show people that God is with us there.
- When you're in the valley, will you focus on the shadow or the shepherd?

PSALM 23

1 The Lord is my shepherd; I shall not want.
2 He makes me lie down in green pastures. He leads me beside still waters. 3 He restores my soul. He leads me in paths of righteousness for his name's sake. 4 Even though I walk through the valley of the shadow of death, I will fear no evil, for you are with me; your rod and your staff, they comfort me. 5 You prepare a table before me in the presence of my enemies; you anoint my head with oil; my cup overflows. 6 Surely goodness and mercy shall follow me all the days of my life, and I shall dwell in the house of the Lord forever.

Rk	Date	Opponent	Result		Passing					Rushing				Total Offense					First Downs			Penalties		Turnovers		
				Cmp	Att	Pct	Yds	TD	Att	Yds	Avg	TD	Plays	Yds	Avg	Pass	Rush	Pen	Tot	No.	Yds	Fum	Int	Tot		
4	9/25/21	@ Vanderbilt	W (62-0)	21	28	75	291	3	45	244	5.4	5	73	535	7.3	14	13	2	29	4	17	0	1	1		

VANDERBILT STADIUM

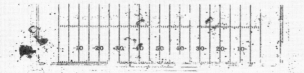

W 62-0
GAME TIME: 12:00 P.M. EST
GAME ATTENDANCE: 32,178

CHAPTER 5

RESILIENCY

ATHENS, GA
OCTOBER 2, 2021

To the choirmaster. A Psalm of David.
1 How long, O Lord? Will you forget me forever?
 How long will you hide your face from me?

2 How long must I take counsel in my soul
 and have sorrow in my heart all the day?
 How long shall my enemy be exalted over me?

3 Consider and answer me, O Lord my God;
 light up my eyes, lest I sleep the sleep of death,

4 lest my enemy say, "I have prevailed over him,"
 lest my foes rejoice because I am shaken.

5 But I have trusted in your steadfast love;
 my heart shall rejoice in your salvation.

6 I will sing to the Lord,
 because he has dealt bountifully with me.

Psalm 13:1-6

Social media has given us more to compare ourselves to than ever before. Over 3 billion images and over 720,000 hours of video are shared online every single day. And with so much comparison happening online, we want the things we post to be perfect. It must have perfect lighting. It must have the perfect angle. We not only want the right music, but we're going to sync the video to make sure the actions and background sound blend perfectly. And sometimes, when we don't like the raw image or video, we will use a filter. Instead of being honest about who we are or even where we are, we use a filter.

Our answer when we don't want to deal with reality is to just slap a filter on it.

There is nothing wrong with using a filter when you are doing something fun or creative. It's an enhancement. But the issue is when the filter causes us to lose sight of reality. That's a problem. Now let's be honest. Some of y'all have slid into the DMs of someone you would eventually meet in person, only to find out that all that glitters is not gold. You encounter someone who is not consistent with what you saw online. If you can understand how frustrating it would be to get one thing online and receive something different in person, then how much more should we understand how frustrating it has to be to know a person who would rather use a filter than accept reality?

There are a lot of us who are way more comfortable with the filter because the filter allows us to escape from reality. Brothers and sisters, when we are resilient that means we are embracing reality. When a person is resilient, they are not just trying to make things look good. Think about the things you most recently posted. Was it real or was it a filter? Maybe you didn't use a filter in the traditional sense, but were those things you posted rooted and grounded in truth? When you posted about how hard you grind, how you are doing it big for the city, or how much you love your family —was it the truth, or was it a filter?

What I love most about the 13th Psalm is that there is no filter. There is no pretty picture presented to make everything look good. In the text, you have a man who is real with God and one who is real with himself. Just so you know the background, the 13th Psalm is connected to David's experience with King Saul. King Saul had failed and fallen off. He had the opportunity to lead, but he wasn't faithful. Therefore, God made a decision to appoint another person!

Catch this — while Saul was still King, David was chosen by God to be the next king, and Saul became jealous. Saul sought to take David out. Now rather than being weak, David was resilient. Rather than trying to use a filter, David chose to be honest with God. David wrote this psalm when he was exhausted and depressed. His fight with King Saul had gone on for years, but he was resilient. People are trying to take his life, and he is tired and weary, but he is honest and resilient. In the psalm, David is facing a challenge. He was facing a trial. He is in a test, and he asked four times how long will it last.

How long?

How long?

How long?

How long?

It is important for us to consider the 13th Psalm because if we are honest, we must confess that we have found ourselves asking the same questions that David is asking. How long will I have to deal with the test? How long will I have to wait? How long will I have to deal with the disappointment? How long, Lord? To me, this psalm is extremely helpful because it reminds us of the reality of walking with God. It reminds me that in a season of difficulty, those who are faithful to God can be honest with God, and they can be honest with others. Those who are faithful to God should not feel the need to fake, perform, or use a filter! We can be honest with God, and we can be honest with others.

In the 13th Psalm, David is willing to do that. And in doing so, David gives us a model for how to be resilient. David gives us a model for how we can deal with the realities of life by being resilient.

First, let us consider David's condition!

1. David's Condition

In scripture, we know that God had promised David the Throne of Israel, yet that day of celebration seemed further and further away. David received a promise from God, but David had to patiently wait for God to fulfill it. Please understand to this point, David has done everything right, but still, he had to wait. He hadn't made any mistakes, but he had to wait. We are willing to wait when we are resilient. When we are resilient, we can trust that the things that God has promised will certainly come to pass.

Statistics show that the average person spends close to an hour every day waiting for something. We wait on elevators. We find ourselves waiting at traffic lights. We wait on our turn to pay at the grocery store. We wait for a table at a restaurant, or we wait for our food after we order. When you add up all of the waiting over a 70-year lifespan, the average person will have spent more than 3 years waiting. The truth is we will have to wait. There is not a person reading this chapter who hasn't had to wait. The problem is not in the waiting. The real problem is what you allow to happen while you wait.

For too many of us, waiting produces impatience rather than perseverance. For many of us, waiting makes us frustrated. Waiting reveals selfishness and anger in our hearts. Here is the truth — while waiting in line, we find flaws with the people in front of us. While waiting, we can pick out the faults of others. How many of us have counted how many items somebody had in the express line ahead of us at the grocery store? We get jealous. We lose focus. All because we have to wait.

What happens in our hearts when God makes us wait?

Let me submit to you that God wants us to live with great expectations. God wants us to live knowing He will supply all of our needs, but we must accept that sometimes God delays His blessings to examine what's in our hearts. God wants us to wait ...on purpose because God is after a purpose greater than our immediate blessing. God doesn't want to just fix our problems. God desires to transform us in the process. So let me ask a question, how are you doing waiting? Remember, in the last chapter, we spoke about serving as a model for others. Specifically, we were encouraged to give a model to follow. When it comes to waiting, what kind of model are you giving?

When my oldest son was born, he was born with a birth defect. Usually, babies are born with a soft open spot in their skulls, but when my son was born, the bones in his skull had completely prematurely fused. His medical condition is called Craniosynostosis. I remember having to wait for the specialist to see him. Then, when we found out he had to have surgery, we had to wait for it to be scheduled. Then, on surgery day, we had to wait for the procedure to be completed. I can remember being in that waiting room, hurting and broken. Then I heard a familiar voice. My good friend from college, Demarco, showed up. He didn't want me to be alone. He saw a need in his brother and came to sit and visit with me. He couldn't change the wait time, but he was willing to be with me while I waited.

Here is the blessing of a team and a family. When I see my brother having to wait, brother, I want to wait with him. While they wait, I want to encourage them. I want to let them know how I made it in the waiting room because another brother did not allow me to wait alone. That's what a team does for one another. That's what a family does for its members.

First, we see David's condition, and then we hear David's cry.

2. David's Cry

3 Consider and answer me, O Lord my God;
light up my eyes, lest I sleep the sleep of death,
4 lest my enemy say, "I have prevailed over him,"
lest my foes rejoice because I am shaken.

The word "shaken" in verse 4 means "to waver, to be agitated, to totter and move". If David began to waver, then the people in the land would think that God was unable to fulfill His promises. David understood that he was representing someone and something greater than himself. Brothers and sisters, do you recognize that what you are representing is way bigger than you? In the text, David is resilient, and he is willing to ask God for help because he has faith that God will answer. Let me just say there is no point in asking unless you are hopeful that someone is listening and that someone can answer. I want to encourage you that while you are waiting, God sees you, God hears you, and God will help you.

But God's help doesn't always look how we expect. God will help, but many times His help can be unexpected. When God helps, He focuses on what we need, not just what we want. God knows what we need. God knows where you are. God also knows where He wants you to be. And God is able to get you there even when you don't see that God is working.

I firmly believe God ordained me to be in this job, but I can honestly say that I didn't go looking for it. God knew where I was, and God knew how to get me here. When I got the call about this job, I was working at a church in Atlanta. I felt like God was moving me away, but I had no idea when, why, or how. So, I just spent time praying. I spent time calling out to God, seeking and asking for wisdom. Then out of nowhere, I got a call from this crazy guy named Chappy. He had posted this job online. Casey Giddeons, a guy I went to seminary with, applied for the position and didn't get it. They declined Casey, and then they asked him if he knew of anyone who would be a good candidate. He gave them my number.

When we call out to God, He will answer. And when He does, we can trust that God is working even if we can't see it!

3. David's Comfort

5 But I have trusted in your steadfast love;
my heart shall rejoice in your salvation.

6 I will sing to the Lord, because he has dealt bountifully with me.

When we read verse 6, we should ask ourselves if David's actual circumstances had changed. There is nothing in the text that suggests it had. There is no direct reference to Saul calling off a manhunt. There is no direct indication that Saul was dead. There is no direct mention of David receiving a new shipment of weapons. But clearly, something changed.

David could sing because God hadn't changed! David's feelings had been on a rollercoaster, but he got to a place where he could trust that God was still in control. David's circumstances hadn't changed, but the

Lord had changed him. Let me say that again. David's circumstances haven't changed, but the Lord has changed him. That change occurred once David stopped focusing on his feelings and his foes, and by faith, David started looking to the Lord.

How different would your life be if you stopped waiting for the circumstances to change? How different would your experience on the team, the job, or the family be if you stopped waiting for the depth chart or the organizational chart to change? How different would you be if you got to the place where you allowed God to change you? When I say that, please know that I'm not saying that the situation is easy. Life rarely is easy. But maybe God wants to use the situation to mold you and shape you to be more like Christ. I love verses 5 and 6 because it helps us to see how we can also experience change. When I shift the focus away from my feelings and away from my foes, so that my focus is on my faith, I will see change!

If you focus on your faith, I can't promise that God will immediately change the tough situation. But there is a promise I can make you. If you focus your attention on your faith and not your feelings and foes, God will change you.

The truth is we can patiently wait on the Lord.

We can passionately and honestly communicate with the Lord.

We can confidently trust in the Lord.

GAME FIVE
DEVOTIONAL CARD

DEVOTIONAL
ATHENS, GA
SATURDAY, OCTOBER 2, 2021

DNA: RESILIENCY

1. DAVID'S CONDITION
- David received a promise from God, but David had to patiently wait on God.
- God uses seasons of waiting to mold us and shape us.

2. DAVID'S CRY
- David prayed for peace within and protection around.
- When David asked for "light," he was seeking God for direction.

3. DAVID'S COMFORT
- David moved from fear to faith.
- David's circumstances didn't change, but the Lord changed him. That occurred when David stopped being ruled by his feelings and foes and started to live by faith.
- What are you ruled by – feelings or faith?

PSALM 13
1 How long, O Lord? Will you forget me forever?
How long will you hide your face from me?
2 How long must I take counsel in my soul
and have sorrow in my heart all the day?
How long shall my enemy be exalted over me?
3 Consider and answer me, O Lord my God;
light up my eyes, lest I sleep the sleep of death,
4 lest my enemy say, "I have prevailed over him,"
lest my foes rejoice because I am shaken.
5 But I have trusted in your steadfast love;
my heart shall rejoice in your salvation.
6 I will sing to the Lord, because he has dealt
bountifully with me.

Rk	Date	Opponent	Result	Passing					Rushing				Total Offense			First Downs				Penalties		Turnovers		
				Cmp	Att	Pct	Yds	TD	Att	Yds	Avg	TD	Plays	Yds	Avg	Pass	Rush	Pen	Tot	No.	Yds	Fum	Int	Tot
5	10/2/21	Arkansas	W (37-0)	7	11	63.6	72	0	56	273	4.9	3	67	345	5.1	3	16	3	22	6	40	0	0	0

SANFORD STADIUM

W 37-0
GAME TIME: 12:00 P.M. EST
GAME ATTENDANCE: 92,746

CHAPTER 6
DEMAND THE STANDARD

AUBURN, AL
OCTOBER 9, 2021

25 "Therefore I tell you, do not be anxious about your life, what you will eat or what you will drink, nor about your body, what you will put on. Is not life more than food, and the body more than clothing? 26 Look at the birds of the air: they neither sow nor reap nor gather into barns, and yet your heavenly Father feeds them. Are you not of more value than they? 27 And which of you by being anxious can add a single hour to his span of life? 28 And why are you anxious about clothing? Consider the lilies of the field, how they grow: they neither toil nor spin, 29 yet I tell you, even Solomon in all his glory was not arrayed like one of these. 30 But if God so clothes the grass of the field, which today is alive and tomorrow is thrown into the oven, will he not much more clothe you, O you of little faith? 31 Therefore do not be anxious, saying, 'What shall we eat?' or 'What shall we drink?' or 'What shall we wear?' 32 For the Gentiles seek after all these things, and your heavenly Father knows that you need them all. 33 But seek first the kingdom of God and his righteousness, and all these things will be added to you. 34 "Therefore do not be anxious about tomorrow, for tomorrow will be anxious for itself. Sufficient for the day is its own trouble.
Matthew 6:25-34

When someone takes a new role or job, they are onboarded or introduced to the organization with an orientation. This is the case for new employment or the beginning of a college career. The orientation process serves as an opportunity for one to find out what he can expect from the organization and what the organization expects from him. The orientation essentially clearly communicates the standard.

Now if we can understand that from an earthly perspective, how much more should we be able to understand that from a spiritual perspective? This morning we are focusing on Matthew chapter 6, which is a part of the Sermon on the Mount. This is probably Jesus' most well-known sermon. In the sermon, Jesus is giving us an orientation into the kingdom. In the sermon, Jesus clearly communicates God's standard of living. In the sermon, Jesus tells us what we can expect from the kingdom of God, and now Jesus is telling us what the kingdom expects from us.

Jesus is giving us a standard.

Now we need to admit that it can be very easy to drift away from the standard. It's easy to let things slip. Think of it this way. Usually, a couple of times a year, we take our cars to the dealership to get them serviced. We need to get the oil changed or to get some other normal maintenance done on our cars. I can remember when I was younger and less knowledgeable about cars. I was one of those guys that would only get my oil changed. While I would never miss an oil change most of the time, I would ignore all the other services that were offered. I wouldn't pay much attention to rotating the tires, changing the air filters, changing the spark plugs, or flushing the fuel systems. In my mind, I didn't need all those recommended services. From my limited perspective, I didn't have enough money or time to focus on those things. However, the wiser I got, the more I began to accept the truth that I needed to listen to what the mechanic was recommending, especially when they told me the car was desperately in need of a realignment.

When the car is out of alignment, it's not operating the way it was designed. When the car is out of alignment, it is not operating based upon a certain standard. When the car is out of alignment, it hurts the gas mileage. It wears out the tires quickly. The ride is not smooth, and most importantly, when the car is out of alignment, it usually drifts too far off-center. The longer the car is out of alignment, the more damage is done to the car. I'm not using this illustration so that you can take your car into the shop. I'm sharing it because it reminds us of the importance of our lives being in alignment with the Lord.

Here is why this is important. I believe we need to ensure that, as a team, we stay in alignment. As a family, we need to be reminded of our standards. Please understand that when a car is out of alignment, it still can be driven; it just won't be able to go as far. A car can be out of alignment and operate, but certain parts of the car are going to wear out quicker. A car can be out of alignment and still drive, but the ride is bumpy and, at times, painful because of the damage that is being done. When I think about it, all of those things can be true of a team, a family, a marriage, or an organization as well.

When we as a team or family are out of alignment, then we are not focused on our why. When we are out of alignment, we are not focused on our mission. When we are not focused on the standard, we can still be a team or a family, but we won't go as far. We can still be a team or a family, but people are going to burn out faster. We can still be a team, but when we are out of alignment, we are not operating the way God created us to operate. So, this morning, I want us to consider our time together as an opportunity to do some realignment. Because when something is out of alignment, it tends to drift.

In the text, Jesus tells us that when we are out of alignment, we are worrying about the wrong things.

1. The Real Reason We Worry

25 *"Therefore I tell you, do not be anxious about your life, what you will eat or what you will drink, nor about your body, what you will put on. Is not life more than food, and the body more than clothing?*

In context, the word anxious means to be unduly concerned. We are challenged not to be anxious. Don't misquote me now. I am not saying that there will never be a time when there is a cause for concern. People get laid off and fired from their jobs. People die. People get injured. There should be some concern. I am not saying there won't be times to be concerned. What I am saying is that there should not be "undue" concern. To be unduly concerned is to neglect the truth that God is in control. When we are unduly concerned, we are worried about the wrong things.

I'm sure everybody reading this devotional has heard of Steve Jobs. Has anybody in here heard of Ronald Wayne? Well, Wayne was the third founder of Apple, but he only lasted two weeks. Steve Jobs had a vision for the company, and he wanted to take out a loan to get some hardware. Wayne was so worried that the loan was only $14,000 that he sold his stake in the company for $800. If he had kept those shares, they would have been worth $98 billion today. When we are unduly concerned, we miss out on opportunities to trust the Lord.

Think for a second about how many opportunities we have missed because we were unduly concerned. How much further along could we be in life, in academics, because we are unduly concerned? When we are unduly concerned, the problem is we take our focus and attention off of God. That is why our attention has to be on God rather than the things of this world. When we read the text, Jesus mentions the world's trinity of cares — what we will eat, what we will drink, and what we will wear. Jesus did not teach us to despise the pleasures of life, but Jesus did challenge us not to possess an unhealthy pursuit of those pleasures. Can we all agree that many times we not only worry, but we worry about things that don't even matter? Here is a question I often ask myself, "Thomas, are you worried about something that will matter in 5 days, 5 months, or 5 years from now?"

Ask yourself the same, and you might be surprised by the answer.

2. The Real Reason Not to Worry

26 Look at the birds of the air: they neither sow nor reap nor gather into barns, and yet your heavenly Father feeds them. Are you not of more value than they? 27 And which of you by being anxious can add a single hour to his span of life? 28 And why are you anxious about clothing? Consider the lilies of the field, how they grow: they neither toil nor spin, 29 yet I tell you, even Solomon in all his glory was not arrayed like one of these. 30 But if God so clothes the grass of the field, which today is alive and tomorrow is thrown into the oven, will he not much more clothe you, O you of little faith?

Why do we have reason not to worry? Because God is not only our Creator and King but also because we are His beloved children. And when we recognize we have a good Father, we have no room to worry. It amazes me how spoiled my kids are for spring break this year. We traveled during this break and had to stay at the hotel. When we got to the hotel, my youngest, Titus, asked me if he could go to the arcade room. I was puzzled. What a strange question. I asked him what he meant by arcade room. He was like, "The room with the video games and the chicken fingers and the babysitters." I was still so confused until it dawned on me. Every time he had ever stayed at a hotel, it was for a Bowl Game! He thought his experience on the Bowl trip would be repeated every time we stayed at a hotel. When I told him that there wasn't an arcade room, he looked at me and asked, "Daddy, why didn't you take us to the other hotel with the game room?" He had gotten to the point of expecting certain things from his father. Because of my job, he has been able to experience life at a certain level, and he has come to expect Dad to provide at that level every time.

Does God provide everything we want? Absolutely not. The lives we live will not be like a Bowl trip or a vacation, but here is what we can expect from God. We can expect that God will supply all of our needs. If God can take care of the birds and the animals, then certainly we can trust that God will take care of us!

The real reason why we don't need to worry is because we have a good God who takes care of everything that we need! Now using that illustration, I'm aware that we all do not have earthly fathers, but we do have a Heavenly Father. As men, we want to aspire to be the kind of earthly father that will build confidence and trust in our Heavenly Father.

The real reason why we worry – we focus on the wrong things. The real reason not to worry – we have a good Father. And lastly, we see the real remedy to worry.

3. The Real Remedy to Worry

31 Therefore do not be anxious, saying, 'What shall we eat?' or 'What shall we drink?' or 'What shall we wear?' 32 For the Gentiles seek after all these things, and your heavenly Father knows that you need them all. 33 But seek first the kingdom of God and his righteousness, and all these things will be added to you. 34 "Therefore do not be anxious about tomorrow, for tomorrow will be anxious for itself. Sufficient for the day is its own trouble.

In the text, Jesus challenges us not to be like the world that is consumed with worry. I love and appreciate Jesus because He doesn't simply diagnose the issue, but He also gives us the remedy. Jesus doesn't desire to be one thing among many. Christ wants to be first.

Have you ever been on a date with a young lady who's more focused on her cell phone than you? She is not paying attention to you. She is operating like the phone is just so important that she can't even pay attention to you. Many of us treat God the same way. Our mindset when it comes to God is that we'll get around to that relationship-with-God stuff later. We need to hear the text clearly. God requests and desires to be first. When the passage says to seek first, it speaks to the priority of God's position. God says to seek Him first, but we usually only consult God when something is broken.

There is a Cosby Show episode where Dr. Huxtable wanted to fix the sink. Claire told him to call the plumber. Theo told him to call the plumber. Vanessa and Rudy told him the same as Theo. Even the neighbor, Bud, told him to call the plumber. Heathcliff just didn't want to listen. But when everything fell apart, he went and called the plumber. If he had just consulted the expert first, then he would have saved time and trouble. If he had just consulted the specialist first then he would have saved money. If he had just consulted the plumber first, then he would have saved himself from the embarrassment, frustration, and anxiety. How many of us can be honest and say that if we had just consulted God first, we could have saved a lot of time, money, and frustration? We try to fix it and it fails.

Here is the standard - we are to go to God first!

33 But seek first the kingdom of God and his righteousness, and all these things will be added to you.

The key to getting what you want out of life is to focus on what God wants for your life. In order to seek the kingdom, you must submit to the

King, that is, Christ, because the King has set the standard.

When people ask me what exactly I do as a chaplain, I tell them a story that I heard a few years ago. A professor wanted to communicate a life-changing principle to his class. So, he went under his desk and pulled out a wide-mouth glass mason jar. The professor then proceeded to place 5 big rocks into the jar. Then he asked his class if, in their estimation, was the jar full. And the entire class responded, yes. After hearing their response, the professor goes back under the table, and this time, he pulls out a bag of gravel. He pours the gravel into the wide-mouth mason jar and then asks them again if it is full. This time about half the class responded, yes. Then the professor goes under the table again and pulls out a bag of sand. He pours it into the wide-mouth mason jar and asks them for a third time if it is full. This time no one in the class responded. So, he asked them why they thought that he put the big rocks in first, then the gravel, and then the sand. No student raised their hand to answer. The professor explained that he put the big rocks in first because that way, everything else would fit.

I told that story because we need to be reminded that God is not simply concerned about our actions, but God is also concerned about the order. In God's design, God has set the standard that He is to always be first.

Tony Evans tells the story of his son dunking a basketball for the first time. Jonathan had been practicing touching the rim for a while, and the day came when he was able to dunk the ball. At age 11, he went and got his father to show his dad that he could finally dunk. Before you get too excited about an 11-year-old dunking, I have got to tell you that Jonathan got tired of trying to reach the standard height, so he had one of the custodians lower the goal. Even though he was able to dunk the ball, his father wasn't pleased because the standard was lowered. Like any good father, I know Dr. Evans raised the rim back to the standard and challenged his son to meet the standard.

That is what God desires for us to do. What the son did is what we are often tempted to do. When times get tough, we want to lower the standard. We often lower the standard of the church. We often lower the standard of marriage. We often lower the standard on how we are to serve the poor or how we are to serve our neighbors. I believe we need to be reminded that rather than lowering the standard, we need to reach for a righteous standard.

Here is how we should operate. No, my marriage may not be perfect, but I'm going to pursue God's standard. No, I'm not going to lower the standard. No, I'm not going to expect the father to be pleased with me lowering the standard.

Coming to church is an important action, but it won't have transformational power unless it's in the right order.

Studying the Scriptures is an important action, but it won't have transformational power unless it's in the right order.

Being involved in a ministry is an important action, but it won't have transformational power unless it's in the right order.

In God's design, God has set the standard that He is to always be first.

DEVOTIONAL
AUBURN, AL
SATURDAY, OCTOBER 9, 2021

DEMAND THE STANDARD

1. THE REAL REASON WHY WE WORRY
- To be anxious means to be unduly concerned.
- The text is not communicating that there will never be a time for concern, but it challenges us to identify undue concern.
- Jesus didn't teach us to despise the pleasures of life. Jesus challenges us not to possess an unhealthy pursuit of those pleasures.

2. THE REAL REASON NOT TO WORRY
- To be unduly concerned is to neglect the truth that God is always in control.
- God is not simply the giver of life but also the sustainer of life.

3. THE REAL REMEDY TO OUR WORRY
- "Seek first the kingdom of God" - speaks to the priority of God's position.
- God is not simply concerned about your actions; He is also concerned about the order.
- The antidote to worrying is having God in His proper position in our lives.

MATTHEW 6

25 "Therefore I tell you, do not be anxious about your life, what you will eat or what you will drink, nor about your body, what you will put on. Is not life more than food, and the body more than clothing? 26 Look at the birds of the air: they neither sow nor reap nor gather into barns, and yet your heavenly Father feeds them. Are you not of more value than they? 27 And which of you by being anxious can add a single hour to his span of life? 28 And why are you anxious about clothing? Consider the lilies of the field, how they grow: they neither toil nor spin, 29 yet I tell you, even Solomon in all his glory was not arrayed like one of these. 30 But if God so clothes the grass of the field, which today is alive and tomorrow is thrown into the oven, will he not much more clothe you, O you of little faith? 31 Therefore do not be anxious, saying, 'What shall we eat?' or 'What shall we drink?' or 'What shall we wear?' 32 For the Gentiles seek after all these things, and your heavenly Father knows that you need them all. 33 But seek first the kingdom of God and his righteousness, and all these things will be added to you. 34 "Therefore do not be anxious about tomorrow, for tomorrow will be anxious for itself. Sufficient for the day is its own trouble.

Rk	Date	Opponent	Result	Passing					Rushing				Total Offense			First Downs				Penalties		Turnovers		
				Cmp	Att	Pct	Yds	TD	Att	Yds	Avg	TD	Plays	Yds	Avg	Pass	Rush	Pen	Tot	No.	Yds	Fum	Int	Tot
6	10/9/21 @ Auburn		W (34-10)	14	21	66.7	231	2	49	201	4.1	2	70	432	6.2	8	11	3	22	3	18	0	0	0

JORDAN-HARE STADIUM

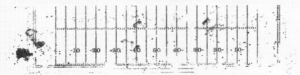

W 34-10
GAME TIME: 3:30 P.M. EST
GAME ATTENDANCE: 87,451

CHAPTER 7
SELF TALK

ATHENS, GA
OCTOBER 16, 2021

1 Bless the Lord, O my soul, and all that is within me, bless his holy name! 2 Bless the Lord, O my soul and forget not all his benefits, 3 who forgives all your iniquity, who heals all your diseases, 4 who redeems your life from the pit, who crowns you with steadfast love and mercy, 5 who satisfies you with good so that your youth is renewed like the eagles. 6 The Lord works righteousness and justice for all who are oppressed. 7 He made known his ways to Moses, his acts to the people of Israel. 8 The Lord is merciful and gracious, slow to anger and abounding in steadfast love.
Psalm 103:1-8

Traditionally being caught talking to yourself can be one of the most embarrassing things ever. Whether you're encouraging yourself to get a task done or critiquing yourself for making a mistake, it's usually uncomfortable to be caught talking to yourself, especially since many of us have come to believe that it is a sign that something is wrong. Many of us have believed that talking to yourself is a sign of something unhealthy. However, according to new research talking to yourself is not only totally normal, but it might actually be helpful. After a series of tests, researchers with the Quarterly Journal of Experimental Psychology concluded that talking to yourself improved not only concentration but also performance. And while we can certainly accept a study from a well-respected academic journal, we must remember that long before university researchers concluded that talking to yourself was healthy, the Lord gave us the 103rd Psalm. I love the 103rd Psalm because David is essentially talking to himself in the first two verses. David declares,

1 Bless the Lord, O my soul and all that is within me, bless his holy name! 2 Bless the Lord, O my soul and forget not all his benefits

Catch the picture. David has his pen in hand. And he is talking to himself about many of the blessings and benefits that accompany a relationship with God. Hear me clearly, David isn't patting himself on the back. David isn't having a pity party. He certainly isn't being prideful, he isn't allowing himself to be held hostage by past success, and he is not overwhelmed with future challenges. But in the Psalm, David encourages himself in the Lord. How does he encourage himself? He encourages himself by talking to himself. David encourages himself by preaching to himself about the Lord. David encourages himself by reminding himself of the truth concerning the Lord. In the text, David is not consumed with his feelings, but he focuses on the facts. He is at a point in his life spiritually where he makes a decision to focus on God's truth rather than man's lies.

Let me submit something to you. In life, yes, it is good to have a preacher in the pulpit on Sunday. Yes, it is good to have a chaplain on gameday. Yes, it is good to get an encouraging text from Mom and Dad. But my brothers and sisters, I want to encourage you that we all need to grow to the place where we can encourage ourselves in the Lord. The way life is set up, every now and then, you might find yourself by yourself, and there are going to be a ton of voices telling you to quit. Voices telling you to leave. Voices telling you that the folks who are trying to help you are really against you. Voices telling you that you have "made it", so you can take it easy. Voices saying that what is in front of you isn't that big of a deal. In those moments, we need to decide to listen to the right voice. Sometimes it's just good to be able to talk to yourself about how good the Lord has been. You won't always be able to get to church. You won't always have a chapel service. You won't always have access to your printed Bible or even your Bible app, and in those moments, it's just good to be able to pause and reflect and preach a sermon to yourself.

That is exactly what takes place in the text. David speaks to himself. David encourages himself by reminding himself of the facts rather than being consumed with his feelings. Essentially, David is giving us a model for how to keep our spiritual fire burning bright. Anyone who has ever been camping knows how important it is not to let the fire go out! I don't know about y'all, but I enjoy watching those survival shows. Just in case you are wondering, the Naked and Afraid show is fake. On

Naked and Afraid, they press pause and bring the doctors in to evaluate you. The real survival show is Alone. If you make it 100 days on the Alone show, you get $1 million. On Alone, they are rooting against you (ha-ha). But, On Naked and Afraid, they are rooting for you. On those shows, one of the first things they do is start a fire. The heat from the fire is absolutely essential for survival. That is also true spiritually. It is easy to lose our passion for the Lord. It is easy to be so focused on the things of this world that the cares and affairs of this world serve as a wet blanket in our lives spiritually. So, if we can understand the importance of keeping a physical fire burning hot. How much more should we understand the need to keep the spiritual fire burning hot?

With any relationship, it is extremely important not to allow the fire to go out! When the fire is dying sometimes you need to add some wood, but other times you need to stir the fire. Here is my point. We need to encourage ourselves in the Lord because that stirs the spiritual fire in our lives. We need to talk to ourselves about how far we have come in our faith. We need to talk to ourselves about the sacrifices that have been made for us to be here. We need to talk to ourselves about our why! Satan is talking! Satan is trying to discourage so we need to join the conversation. In our lives spiritually, we have got to understand the need to be stirred up. When our spiritual fire is dying down. We need to stir it up with the Word, with prayer, with worship, with fellowship, and with discipleship!

This is true for every believer. In our text, David has his pen in hand, and he is about to catalog some of the many and matchless blessings from God that he has experienced. David preaches to himself about God's miracle, David preaches to himself about God's mercy, and lastly, David preaches to himself about God's majesty.

First, let's consider God's miracle.

1. David Speaks to Himself about God's Miracle.

3 who forgives all your iniquity, who heals all your diseases, 4 who redeems your life from the pit, who crowns you with steadfast love and mercy, 5 who satisfies you with good so that your youth is renewed like the eagles. 6 The Lord works righteousness and justice for all who are oppressed. 7 He made known his ways to Moses, his acts to the people of Israel.

One of my mentors, Robert Smith Jr., often says "A man of God is simply a miracle wrapped up in a mess." Let me repeat that, "A man of God or a woman of God is simply a miracle wrapped up in a mess." The miracle is not that we are perfect, but that we are sinful and God still cares for us. The miracle is that God does not give up on us. There is no doubt about it. David was a man of God. The Bible actually describes him as a man after God's own heart. Even though this was true, there were still times in his life when he found himself in a mess. There were times in his life when he got comfortable, where he lost focus, where he messed up, but God got him out of that mess. He was a man of God, but he found himself in a mess. I love highlighting the fact that he found himself in a mess because it is a reminder that we don't always have to be in that mess. We might find ourselves in a mess, but we don't have to stay in the mess. Listen to me. Just because you find yourself in a mess doesn't mean that you have to stay in the mess. Satan desires for us to believe that we are who we are and that we will never change. Satan wants you to believe that the way things are is the way things always will be, that things are the way they are, and that things won't ever change.

Let me help you out.

That's a lie! That kind of mindset is a part of Satan's plan to hold you hostage spiritually. I love our passage because David is an example of how and why God gets us out of the mess. David knew that he didn't have to stay in the mess because he had been forgiven. Rather than focus on his past failures, David chooses to focus on God's present forgiveness because he understood what God desired. Rather than just bringing money, giving his gifts, or donating time, David made the decision to offer a thankful heart and a bold declaration about the blessings and benefits of our God.

When you get to verse 3 you see David declaring the goodness of God because of God's forgiveness

3 who forgives all your iniquity,

God has forgiven all our iniquities. Iniquities are not simply mistakes. Jesus simply didn't die for a mistake, Jesus died for our sins! Get the picture here. In the passage, it is as if David is painting the picture of a courtroom. Satan is called the accuser of the brethren, and oftentimes, Satan will accuse us of lies, but other times Satan will also accuse us of the truth. Satan reminds us of the sin in our lives. Satan is quick to remind us of that time when we had too much to drink, and that was the truth. Satan is quick to remind us of that time when we logged onto that pornographic site, and that is the truth. Satan is quick to remind us of the times we failed or of that time when we were envious of a brother or sister, and that was the truth. Satan lies, but sometimes he will attack you with the truth. That is why forgiveness is so powerful. Though Satan serves as our adversary, Jesus serves as our advocate. One preacher said it this way... "Every time Satan brings a charge against the elect, Jesus raises his nail-pierced hands, and sins are forgiven." David talks to himself about the Miracle of forgiveness because David knew he was guilty. He, like us, needed that reminder.

First, David speaks to himself about God's miracle. Secondly, he speaks to himself about God's mercy.

2. David Speaks to Himself about God's Mercy.

8 The Lord is merciful and gracious,   slow to anger and abounding in steadfast love. 9 He will not always chide, nor will he keep his anger forever. 10 He does not deal with us according to our sins, nor repay us according to our iniquities.

When you read verses 8-10, it is clear that the passage is communicating that God gives us mercy. David certainly addresses grace and how God gives us what we don't deserve, but now he takes the time to address mercy. Do you know the difference between grace and mercy? When we speak about mercy, I'm specifically addressing how God withholds what we deserve.

I remember the first time I understood mercy. I played a lot of baseball growing up and enjoyed throwing the ball with my friends. My mom told me many times "Boy, don't throw that baseball near my house. If you break my window, I'm going to break you." I didn't listen. I remember throwing a baseball with my friend, Michael Godard. Mike threw it high, and it hit the window. It's one thing to see my fate in that broken glass, but it was only about noon when it happened. So, all day, my sisters kept saying how mom was going to "get me" when she returned home. So, I made a decision that I was going to meet my mom at the door with a belt and confess my sins before she even saw the broken glass. Because I confessed, my mom gave me grace on that day. It taught me a great lesson about mercy. In the passage, there is a significant promise. Let's consider verse 10 again.

10 He does not deal with us according to our sins, nor repay us according to our iniquities.

Did you understand that? God does not deal with us according to our sins. Nor repay us according to our iniquities. I know we want to hear that God promises to give us whatever we want. I know we want to hear that God promises to keep us. I know we want to hear that God promises to bless us and punish anyone who is against us, but trust me when I say that the passage gives us a far more significant promise than anything I just mentioned. God promises to not repay us for our iniquities. Do you understand what a phenomenal promise that is from God? God has every right to deal with you and me according to our sins. God has every right to repay you for your iniquity, but God says I'm not going to do that.

That's why it's mercy! Don't miss this! Rather than failing to acknowledge how God shows us mercy, should we not show the same mercy to others?

And since God has chosen to manifest his mercy in my life, should I not show mercy to those in my life? I mean, I could deal with people according to their sins. I could deal with people according to their mistakes. I could beat them down because they failed to reach a standard that I have set, but in light of how God relates to me, that is how I should relate to others. Don't mishear me. David experienced mercy because he possessed a repentant heart. There was reconciliation with God after there was repentance. There was a turning back to God. If we hold sin, or if we become hard-hearted, then God won't hear from us.

Here is how I apply the truth of the passage. Since God does not beat me down and continuously focus on my faults, should I not take the same approach and show mercy to the people God has planted in my life? We need to understand that it is mercy because God withholds what he should give us. Some of us need to hear that today. That God is not waiting to zap you or strike you down when you sin. I'm not preaching easy believe-ism where you can just do whatever you want to do all the time, any time. But I'm preaching the gospel, which reminds us that God's love for us is steadfast and consistent. Part of the reason why we have so much trouble believing this truth is because we do the complete opposite. We consistently repay evil with evil, and our love is anything but steadfast and consistent. But God is manifest in His mercy!

From the miracle to the mercy, David preaches to himself about God's majesty.

3. David Speaks to Himself about God's Majesty.

19 The Lord has established his throne in the heavens, and his kingdom rules over all. 20 Bless the Lord, O you his angels, you mighty ones who do his word, obeying the voice of his word! 21 Bless the Lord, all his hosts, his ministers, who do his will! 22 Bless the Lord, all his works, in all places of his dominion. Bless the Lord, O my soul!

When we read verses 19-22, it is clear that wherever God's dominion is to be found, praise should be offered. And since there is no corner or crevice of the universe where God's dominion can't be found, there should be no corner or crevice where praise is not found. That is why we are here; we want to offer praise to the One who is worthy. That's why we invite friends to church. We want praise to be offered to the One who is worthy. That's why we give to missions. We want praise to be offered to the One who is worthy. That's why we want to grow in our faith, make disciples, and live out the gospel, or get that degree. We want praise to be offered to the One who is worthy.

Think about it this way. Close your eyes and imagine that today is your payday. You have worked hard. You have earned your check. You have done everything they have asked you to do, and you log onto your account, and that direct deposit is missing. That payment hasn't been processed. How are you going to feel? What thoughts will you have? Open up your eyes. If you understand how it would be frustrating not to receive what you are owed, then on a much grander and important level, how should we feel when we fail to offer God what is due?

So let me be clear. The passage is communicating that wherever God's dominion is to be found, praise should be offered. Since there is no corner or crevice of the universe where God's dominion can't be found, there should be no corner or crevice where praise is not found.

Because of God's miracle, we have a right to bless the Lord.

Because of God's mercy, we have a reason to bless the Lord.

God is not waiting to deal with us based on our mistakes. God deals with us according to His steadfast love. And because of God's majesty, we have a responsibility to bless the Lord! We owe God our praise — because it is due!

PRE-GAME CHAPEL
ATHENS, GA
SATURDAY, OCTOBER 16, 2021

SELF - TALK

1. DAVID SPEAKS TO HIMSELF ABOUT GOD'S MIRACLE
- It has been said that "a man is simply a mess wrapped in a miracle". Even though David was a man after God's own heart, he found himself in a mess.
- We might find in ourselves in a mess, but we don't have to stay there.
- Rather than focusing on past failures, David focused on present forgiveness.

2. DAVID SPEAKS TO HIMSELF ABOUT GOD'S MERCY
- David certainly addresses grace - how God gives us what we don't deserve; but he also takes the time to address mercy - how God withholds what we do deserve.
- God promises not to repay us for our sins.
- Since God shows me mercy – I should show that same mercy to others.

3. DAVID SPEAKS TO HIMSELF ABOUT GOD'S MAJESTY
- Wherever God's dominion is to be found - praise should be offered.
- We should desire to offer praise to the only one who is worthy of it.
- Because of God's miracle we have a right to bless the Lord. Because of God's mercy we have a reason to bless the Lord. Because of God's majesty we have a responsibility to bless the Lord!

PSALM 103

1 Bless the Lord, O my soul, and all that is within me, bless his holy name! 2 Bless the Lord, O my soul and forget not all his benefits, 3 who forgives all your iniquity, who heals all your diseases, 4 who redeems your life from the pit, who crowns you with steadfast love and mercy, 5 who satisfies you with good so that your youth is renewed like the eagle's. 6 The Lord works righteousness and justice for all who are oppressed. 7 He made known his ways to Moses, his acts to the people of Israel. 8 The Lord is merciful and gracious, slow to anger and abounding in steadfast love.

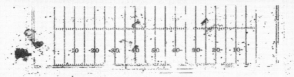

W 30-13
GAME TIME: 3:30 P.M. EST
GAME ATTENDANCE: 92,746

Rk	Date	Opponent:	Result	Passing					Rushing				Total Offense			First Downs				Penalties		Turnovers		
				Cmp	Att	Pct	Yds	TD	Att	Yds	Avg	TD	Plays	Yds	Avg	Pass	Rush	Pen	Tot	No.	Yds	Fum	Int	Tot
7	10/16/21	Kentucky	W (30-13)	14	20	70	250	3	27	166	6.1	1	47	416	8.9	13	7	0	20	5	42	0	0	0

SANFORD STADIUM

CHAPTER 8
HELP OTHERS WIN

JACKSONVILLE, FL
OCTOBER 30, 2021

7 Do not waste time arguing over godless ideas and old wives' tales. Instead, train yourself to be godly. 8 "Physical training is good, but training for godliness is much better, promising benefits in this life and in the life to come." 9 This is a trustworthy saying, and everyone should accept it. 10 This is why we work hard and continue to struggle, for our hope is in the living God, who is the Savior of all people and particularly of all believers.11 Teach these things and insist that everyone learn them. 12 Don't let anyone think less of you because you are young. Be an example to all believers in what you say, in the way you live, in your love, your faith, and your purity. 13 Until I get there, focus on reading the Scriptures to the church, encouraging the believers, and teaching them.14 Do not neglect the spiritual gift you received through the prophecy spoken over you when the elders of the church laid their hands on you. 15 Give your complete attention to these matters. Throw yourself into your tasks so that everyone will see your progress. 16 Keep a close watch on how you live and on your teaching. Stay true to what is right for the sake of your own salvation and the salvation of those who hear you.
1 Timothy 4: 7 -16

Most of you guys don't know the name John Browne, but I guarantee John Browne knows most of you guys by name. Due to the separation of Church and State, I am not employed by the university, but I am employed by a ministry. John is one of my biggest supporters. John is a part of the board that helps me raise my salary. I am a missionary, which means people give money so I can do ministry. Because of COVID, we had to cancel our fundraising gala as well as the event held at his house annually. But because John loves and believes in me, he has been doing all he can to help me raise money. So much so that for his 50th birthday, John told everyone to not bring him a gift. He told everyone to give to this ministry. Rather than receiving something on his birthday, a day designated to celebrate him, he decided to encourage everyone to give to my ministry. Why in the world would someone do that?

John is not just committed to seeing me win, but John wants the men in this room to win too. John wants the men in this room to grow. John wants the men in this room to be blessed. Is John committed to winning personally? Of course, he is. He is leading a great company. He has a beautiful wife, Carrie, and they've been blessed with three amazing daughters. John has a gorgeous home and lives a very blessed life. But John has gotten to the point in his life where he has concluded that it is not enough for him to simply win. This is his mindset — *it's not enough for me and my family to win*. He is living and operating in a way that it's clear that he wants others to win too! There is a proverb that says, "If you want happiness for an hour, take a nap. If you want happiness for a day, go on a trip. If you want happiness for a year, inherit a fortune. But if you want happiness for a lifetime, help somebody."

One of the blessings of my serving as a chaplain for so long is the relationships that I have seen. I remember when AJ Green got to campus. Mohamed Massaquoi was a senior, and yes, they competed against each other fiercely. But I if were to call AJ right now, he would tell you Mohamed helped him win. When Sony Michel and Nick Chubb got to UGA — Todd Gurley was the man. Yes, they, too, competed heavily, but if you called Nick and Sony, they would tell you without missing a beat that Todd helped them win. When D'Andre Swift got to campus, Nick and Sony were the lead dawgs, but if you called Swift right now, he would tell you that Sony and Nick helped him win.

Who on this team are you helping win? Who in your community, family, church, or job are you committed to helping win? Who in your life will be able to say you taught them how to win? In practice, you taught them how to win. At Rankin the academic center, you taught them how to win. After football was over, you taught them how to win. Think for a second, what is something you want to personally accomplish? Take some time, write down those goals, and ask God to empower you to reach them. I love hearing about personal goals, but I also want us to consider what we are helping others accomplish.

I know you want to accomplish something special, but how often do you think about helping others win? What are you willing to give up? What things are you willing to personally change to help others win? What things in your life will increase? And what things in your life will cease so that you can help others win?

That's really the mindset of our passage. Paul has had a very successful season of ministry, but that season is coming to an end. As Paul is writing the letter, he clearly has more years behind him than in front of him. Rather than bragging about himself or reminding his young protégé of all he had accomplished, he takes the time to help someone else win. Paul was the leader, and Timothy was the apprentice. Paul was like the 5th-year senior, and Timothy was like the talented freshman.

One of my favorite preachers says it this way, he says we all need a Paul in our lives. We need someone to challenge us, we need someone to encourage us, we need someone to hold us accountable, but in addition to needing a Paul, we also need a Timothy. We need someone in our lives who we are investing in. We need someone who we can encourage. We need someone who we can be real with about our mistakes and our weaknesses. We need someone who can stand on our shoulders so they go further and farther than us.

I know we have a big game today, but do you have a Paul in your life? Someone that you have given the green light to challenge you. Someone who is a few stages ahead of you? Someone who is where you want to be? Not someone who is perfect, but someone you respect? In addition to needing a Paul in your life, I believe that you also need a Timothy in your life. Someone who you are as committed to seeing win as yourself. Someone who you are as committed to being successful as yourself. Here is the great thing about Paul, his season was almost over, but he was just as concerned about Timothy growing as he was himself. And because Paul was faithful and committed, he took the time to pass the leadership baton to Timothy, and he told him if you are going to lead well, then you need to invest well.

In our text, Paul gives us three things that will help us win in life.

1. **Be Disciplined (v.7).**

⁷ Do not waste time arguing over godless ideas and old wives' tales. Instead, train yourself to be godly.

God gives us some great and gracious gifts. We have the gift of salvation. We have the gift of athletic ability. We have the gift of truth in God's word. One of the most neglected gifts that God has given us is time. Time is one of the most neglected gifts because time is a gift that we often waste. Time is one of God's greatest gifts to us because what we do with our time is our gift back to Him. In the text, Paul is saying one of the worst ways to waste your time is to entertain other people's opinions. The passage is communicating that if you want to waste time, then take the time to listen to what people have to say. If that is true, then the opposite must also be true. If you want to protect your time, then don't be bothered by people's opinions. The reference to "ideas & old wives' tales" is a reminder that the opinions of man should never be as important as God's truth!

If you look on social media, you'll see men and women weighing on every topic under the sun. You'll find opinions about music. You'll find opinions about movies, shows, and pop culture. You'll see opinions about fashion. You'll find strong opinions about celebrity culture and who should or should not be dating. In the grand scheme of things, those opinions don't matter. Your opinion about Lebron doesn't matter to Lebron. Your opinion about Beyonce or Taylor Swift doesn't matter to them. In the text, Paul is reminding Timothy that people's opinions should never be important. In the game today, the fans have an opinion. The other coaches have an opinion. The other players have an opinion, but in this life, we would do well to be reminded that none of those opinions will ever matter.

Paul says the opinions of people should never matter. But then Paul reminds Timothy of what really matters. What God says about us is truth, and that absolutely matters. Let me ask you a question. When God sees you, what do you think he sees? Do you see God as being angry with you? Do you see God as being upset with you? Is God looking down at you thinking, "Man you need to get your stuff together!"

Last weekend on Sunday, my son's team won their 8th game this year. He had two tackles. He didn't play as much as I wanted him to, but my dad was there. His siblings were there also. After the game, we all took him out to eat in celebration, not because of how he performed in the game, but because of his position in my life. I don't love my son based on his performance. I love him based on his position in my life. My son has figured out he will always have a cheering section and win or lose, we are going to celebrate him because he belongs to us! Whether you are a coach, player, parent, or fan, what God says about you does not change based on your performance. God deals with you based on your position. When you become a believer, God does not deal with us according to our sins. Because of grace, God sees himself when He sees us. And what God says about us is that we are forgiven, redeemed, blessed, confident, and powerful!

In the text, we are told about a new position we possess in Christ. But Paul also speaks about practice. He says bodily exercise benefits us only during this life, but training for godliness is much better because it benefits this life as well as the life to come.

So, I got myself an Apple watch and I do Apple Fitness. The workouts are benefiting me. They are hard, but it is worth it. Spiritual exercising is hard, but it is worth it too. Spending time in God's word is hard, but it's worth it. Getting up tomorrow to go to church is hard. but it is worth it. Not putting certain things in your body is hard, but worth it. Cutting unhealthy people out of your life is hard, but it's worth it. Please don't miss this. Paul did not ask Timothy to choose between the two because God expects us to practice both. Here is the truth. We should not invest more into a game than we do in our relationship with God. We should not invest more in our careers than we do in our relationship with God. We want our relations with God to be of the utmost importance.

Paul encourages Timothy to be disciplined, but he also encourages him to be devoted.

2. **Be Devoted (v.12).**

12 Don't let anyone think less of you because you are young. Be an example to all believers in what you say, in the way you live, in your love, your faith, and your purity.

At the time that this was written, Timothy was probably between the ages of 18 to 21. Now because he was young and gifted, there were tons of people watching his life. Some were supportive. Some were rooting for him while others were just waiting and watching for the moment that he would fail.

Since Timothy had so much attention, Paul encouraged him to live in such a way that no one could question his commitment. We are called to be examples in our speech of what we say. Will we speak life or speak death? The Bible says life and death are in the power of the tongue. After our speech, he addressed our conduct and the application of what we say. He says saying the right thing is not enough. You must do what is right also. If the coach calls in a signal, it is not enough for you to simply call out the right play. We need you to execute the right play also. Paul addresses our speech, our conduct, but also our love — the motivation for what we say. For many of us, love for self is our greatest motivation, and I think that is wrong. Love for others must always be a greater motivation. When I was playing ball in college, my position coach would always say, "The big eye in the sky, don't lie:" If someone watched your life like we watch game film, what would they consistently see? In our speech, conduct, and love, we must be disciplined and devoted.

3. **Be Diligent (v. 14)**

14 Do not neglect the spiritual gift you received through the prophecy spoken over you when the elders of the church laid their hands on you. 15 Give your complete attention to these matters. Throw yourself into your tasks so that everyone will see your progress.

Here is what the passage is communicating. Don't hold back. Throw yourself into it. Be all in all. Don't have a way; go all the way. Catch this. If you don't go all in, how can you expect those who are with you to be all in? No one can lead people where they have never been themselves. The word *gift* is the Greek word charisma. It simply means "a gracious gift from God."

Usually, on a person's birthday, they receive a cake. We love the finished product of the cake, but we must recognize that it takes a lot of bitter ingredients to make something sweet. But there is an involved process to finish the cake. Without the eggs, the cake wouldn't hold together. Without the flour, the cake would not have substance. Without the salt, the cake wouldn't have the right flavor. Without the butter, the cake wouldn't be moist. And without the heat, the cake wouldn't rise. But to bake a cake that you can enjoy, you need all of that. To be a great team, you need the bitter parts to make the season sweet. We need Bloody Tuesday. We need Rankin. We need the weight room. We need one real session, and we even need people hating on us and doubting us. Because it makes the cake even more sweet!

There is nothing more important than the responsibilities we have been given by God.

DEVOTIONAL
JACKSONVILLE, FL
SATURDAY, OCTOBER 30, 2021

HELP OTHERS WIN

1. BE DISCIPLINED
- Time is one of God's gifts to us. What we do with it is a gift back to Him.
- The reference to "ideas & old wives' tales" is a reminder that people's opinions should never be important.
- Bodily exercise benefits us only during this life. Godly exercise is profitable now and for eternity. Paul did not ask Timothy to choose between the two because God expects us to practice both.

2. BE DEVOTED
- Paul encouraged Timothy to live in such a way that no one could question his commitment.
- We are called to be examples in our speech, conduct, love, faith & purity.
- The big eye in the sky don't lie: If someone watched your life – like we watch film – what would they consistently see?

3. BE DILIGENT
- No one can lead people where they have never been themselves.
- The word "gift" is the Greek word *charisma*; meaning "a gracious gift from God."
- There is nothing more important than gifts and responsibilities we have been given by God.

1 Timothy 4

7 Do not waste time arguing over godless ideas and old wives' tales. Instead, train yourself to be godly. 8 "Physical training is good, but training for godliness is much better, promising benefits in this life and in the life to come." 9 This is a trustworthy saying, and everyone should accept it. 10 This is why we work hard and continue to struggle, for our hope is in the living God, who is the Savior of all people and particularly of all believers. 11 Teach these things and insist that everyone learn them. 12 Don't let anyone think less of you because you are young. Be an example to all believers in what you say, in the way you live, in your love, your faith, and your purity. 13 Until I get there, focus on reading the Scriptures to the church, encouraging the believers, and teaching them. 14 Do not neglect the spiritual gift you received through the prophecy spoken over you when the elders of the church laid their hands on you. 15 Give your complete attention to these matters. Throw yourself into your tasks so that everyone will see your progress. 16 Keep a close watch on how you live and on your teaching. Stay true to what is right for the sake of your own salvation and the salvation of those who hear you.

Rk	Date	Opponent	Result	Passing					Rushing				Total Offense			First Downs				Penalties		Turnovers		
				Cmp	Att	Pct	Yds	TD	Att	Yds	Avg	TD	Plays	Yds	Avg	Pass	Rush	Pen	Tot	No.	Yds	Fum	Int	Tot
8	10/30/21	N. Florida	W (34-7)	10	19	52.6	161	1	33	193	5.8	2	52	354	6.8	7	10	1	18	6	38	1	2	3

TIAA BANK FIELD

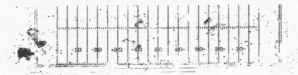

W 34-7

GAME TIME: 3:30 P.M. EST
GAME ATTENDANCE: 76,141

CHAPTER 9
HUMILITY

ATHENS, GA
NOVEMBER 6, 2021

1 So if there is any encouragement in Christ, any comfort from love, any participation in the Spirit, any affection and sympathy, 2 complete my joy by being of the same mind, having the same love, being in full accord and of one mind. 3 Do nothing from selfish ambition or conceit, but in humility count others more significant than yourselves. 4 Let each of you look not only to his own interests, but also to the interests of others. 5 Have this mind among yourselves, which is yours in Christ Jesus, 6 who, though he was in the form of God, did not count equality with God a thing to be grasped, 7 but emptied himself, by taking the form of a servant, being born in the likeness of men. 8 And being found in human form, he humbled himself by becoming obedient to the point of death, even death on a cross. 9 Therefore God has highly exalted him and bestowed on him the name that is above every name, 10 so that at the name of Jesus every knee should bow, in heaven and on earth and under the earth, 11 and every tongue confess that Jesus Christ is Lord, to the glory of God the Father.
Philippians 2:1 -11

There is a story told about a reporter who wanted to chronicle the sacrifices of individuals who went to war. In particular, the reporter wanted to feature individuals who were severely injured. While visiting a VA hospital the reporter met a man who lost his arm during combat. Rather than jumping right in and asking questions, the reporter said, "Thank you for your service. You lost your arm fighting for a great cause."

The soldier quickly responded, "No sir, I didn't lose my arm." He continued, "When I signed up for the military, I signed up to sacrifice my life for my country. Sir, I didn't lose my arm. I gave it in service to my country."

Think for a second about your time being on this team. Would you say that by being on this team you are losing something or are you giving something? Pause for a second tonight, are you losing an opportunity to go downtown or are you giving your focus so that you can be as prepared as possible? Wherever you are in life, are you losing something or are you giving something? Are you losing an opportunity to party or are you giving your life to investing in your family?

I love that opening story because it is a reminder that when Christ went to the Cross, He didn't lose his life. Christ ultimately gave his life so that we could have life. That is why Mark 10:45 clearly states that Jesus came not to be served but to serve and to give his life as a ransom for many. The life of Jesus is marked by humility.

I think it's important that we be reminded that when Paul wrote the Book of Philippians from prison. In a way, you can say he has been quarantined with a group of criminals. He is isolated and alone, but the Apostle Paul still has joy. Paul is in prison, but he still possesses joy. Paul is in prison, but he still possesses peace. Paul is in prison, but he still possesses the right perspective. And the perspective that he possessed caused him to be more concerned about others than himself. I saw a quote this week from Cordarrelle Patterson who is playing for the Falcons right now. At the moment, he is playing three positions, and they asked him how he was able to do that. He responded, "Man, if my momma can work three jobs to put food on the table, then I can easily play three positions to help my team." He saw the sacrifice of his momma and that made him want to make sacrifices. He saw everything that his momma had done and that made him want to do more. Now on a higher and much more important level, Paul understands the sacrifice of Christ, and seeing His sacrifice got him to a place in his life where he was willing to be humble. He saw the humility of Christ, and that led him to be humble.

The attitude that Paul possessed is an attitude that we should all possess if we are a part of the family of God. I love the passage because it is powerful in its implications and direction. Paul doesn't simply tell us to be humble, but he takes it a step further. He takes time to describe what it looks like when we are humble.

The first thing that Paul says is that humility helps us focus on unity.

1. Humility Helps Us Focus on Unity.

2:1 So if there is any encouragement in Christ, any comfort from love, any participation in the Spirit, any affection and sympathy, 2 complete my joy by being of the same mind, having the same love, being in full accord and of one mind.

In verse 2, Paul says something significant when he says, " Complete my joy". We are specifically being told what gives Jesus joy. Think for a second. What brings you joy? We are told specifically what brings Jesus joy. Please don't miss that. In the text, Paul asks if there is a way for Christians to be encouraged. Is there a way for Christians to find comfort? Is there a way for Christians to share in the ministry of the Holy Spirit? If there is a way for Christians to show compassion, it can only happen through unity.

Since encouragement and compassion can only be experienced through unity, then the opposite must also be true. Where there is no unity, there can be no comfort. Where there is no unity, there can be no encouragement. Where there is no unity, there can be no compassion. Unity is absolutely essential in the body of Christ.

As I studied our passage in Philippians this morning, I could not help but think of Jesus's prayer for the church in *John 17.*

9 I am praying for them. I am not praying for the world but for those whom you have given me, for they are yours. 10 All mine are yours, and yours are mine, and I am glorified in them. 11 And I am no longer in the world, but they are in the world, and I am coming to you. Holy Father, keep them in your name, which you have given me, that they may be one, even as we are one. 12 While I was with them, I kept them in your name, which you have given me. I have guarded them, and not one of them has been lost except the son of destruction, that the Scripture might be fulfilled. 13 But now I am coming to you, and these things I speak in the world, that they may have my joy fulfilled in themselves.20 "I do not ask for these only, but also for those who will believe in me through their word, 21 that they may all be one, just as you, Father, are in me, and I in you, that they also may be in us, so that the world may believe that you have sent me. 22 The glory that you have given me I have given to them, that they may be one even as we are one, 23 I in them and you in me, that they may become perfectly one, so that the world may know that you sent me and loved them even as you loved me.

When we are humble, we accept that God wants us to be together. When we are humble, we accept that we are able to accomplish more together, than separately. Consider this — on July 2nd, 1962, a small convenience store was opened up in Rogers, Arkansas. There was not a major grand opening. There was no one from the press or local media present. There was not a national launch or promotional push, just a simple opening by an entrepreneur with a vision of building an empire. Today, that small convenience store is known as the world's largest company by revenue and the largest private employer in the world, with 2.2 million employees. What started in Rogers, Arkansas, has literally expanded across the world. On July 2nd, 1962 I don't believe anyone could have imagined the scope and the scale that this man's store would one day reach!

On a much more significant level, I don't believe we understand how much we can accomplish together. Humility says we can do more together than we can ever do separately. Reflecting on this issue of love for one another in church, Thomas Manton says, "Divisions in the church breed atheism in the world." If that statement is true, then the opposite should also be. Unity in the church builds belief in the world. This is also true on our team. Belief in the team builds belief in the world. If you don't think unity and connection are important, then I want you to consider the following. The quickest way to kill a part of your body is to cut it off from the rest of your body. If you can kill a finger, cut it off from a hand. If you want to kill a foot, cut it off from a leg. Sometimes we think we should do our own thing, but the truth is we need to be connected. Unity not only blesses the team, but it blesses us!

First, Paul tells us that humility helps us focus on unity. However, secondly, Paul tells us that humility helps us focus on our responsibility.

2. Humility Helps Us Focus on Our Responsibility.

3 Do nothing from selfish ambition or conceit, but in humility count others more significant than yourselves. 4 Let each of you look not only to his own interests, but also to the interests of others.

Reading these verses, I am reminded that there is a huge difference between entitlement and responsibility. An entitlement mindset says certain things are owed to me. The scholarship check is owed to me. The catered food is owed to me. The gear is owed to me. The new facility is owed to me. Entitlement focuses on what we feel is owed to us while responsibility looks at things from a different perspective. Responsibility says I have been given this opportunity, and I want to take advantage of it. Responsibility says I want to be found faithful over the opportunity. Responsibility says I want to take care of all the blessings. I am going to take care of the scholarship check. I am going to take care of the facility. I am going to take care of the team because this is a responsibility that I have been given by God.

Paul is saying we don't look out for our own interests first because we are following the attitude and example of Christ. Jesus did not look out for his own self-interest. It has been said that Paul's formula for joy stands out in Philippians. It is J (Jesus), O (Others), Y (Yourself). So very often, we try to have Paul's joy while we reverse his formula. It cannot be done. We can't spell "joy" by putting the Y first, and we can't find joy by putting ourselves first.

7 but emptied himself, by taking the form of a servant being born in the likeness of men. 8 And being found in human form, he humbled himself by becoming obedient to the point of death, even death on a cross.

When we read verses 7 and 8, we need to remember that Christ did not give up His deity. He made himself of no reputation not by the subtraction of divinity but by the addition of humanity. The English commentator BB Warfield says,

"The Lord of the world became a servant in the world; He whose right it was to rule took obedience as His life-characteristic." Look at Christ there taking the very form of a servant in human likeness. He became what he had never been before without ceasing to be what he had always been. He chose to be born as a baby. He chose to live as a man, suffer as an outcast, and die as a criminal. He traded the homage and adoration of angels for the hatred of man. He remained everything involved in being God, and at the same time, he became everything involved in being a man.

As we read the passage, we should read these words with a sense of awe and wonder. If anyone ever had the right to insist on his rights, it was the Lord Jesus. But His concern for others was so important that He refused to insist on his rights. He did not cling to his divine prerogatives, but willingly laid aside all His rights and took our humanity. When we begin to understand the attitude of Christ, it should make us humble.

Here we have Jesus leaving heaven and forgiving us of our sins, and we can't even forgive someone for not returning our phone call. Here we have the attitude of Christ seeking to restore, and we are holding grudges. We say things like:

"If he thinks I'm going to ever trust him again, he's crazy."

"If they think I'm going to admit my faults, they are stupid."

And all the while, we have Christ laying aside his rights so that we can have a relationship with him.

Shame on us. Someone might be reading this devotional thinking *ok I get the point, but how am I going to show humility in my life?*

How does Christ show humility? The text gives us two ways, and the first way is through service. Jesus serves (Phil. 2:7). Because only thinking of others in a theoretical sense is not good enough. There is a story told about a missionary who was attending a religious festival in Brazil. The missionary was going from booth to booth, taking in the festival. As he enjoyed the festival, he saw a sign above one booth that read "Cheap Crosses." He thought to himself, "That's what many Christians are looking for these days — cheap crosses." Our Lord's cross was not cheap. And your cross won't be either!

Any believer with a Christ-like attitude does not avoid sacrifice. It was Christ's attitude. It was Paul's attitude, and it should be our attitude. As much as we hate to admit it, sacrifice and service go together if we are going to be faithful to the Lord.

It is one of the paradoxes of the Christian life that the more we serve and give things away, the more the Lord allows us to receive.

This is how an attitude like Christ leads to joy.

Think about it this way: what is it costing you to follow Christ?

Humility helps us focus on unity.

Humility helps us focus on our responsibility.

Humility helps us focus on eternity.

3. A Christ-like Attitude is Always Focused on Eternity.

9 Therefore God has highly exalted him and bestowed on him the name that is above every name, 10 so that at the name of Jesus every knee should bow, in heaven and on earth and under the earth, 11 and every tongue confess that Jesus Christ is Lord, to the glory of God the Father.

The things that you do will speak for you when you are gone, but the things that we do also matter in eternity. The things you do for Christ will leave a legacy.

Think about being a senior on your favorite collegiate team. Your eligibility is up. Your time is done. If someone were to review the tape, what would you leave as a legacy?

What have you done for Christ and others that will matter in eternity? Live your life — a life in humility — with this in mind.

DEVOTIONAL
ATHENS, GA
SATURDAY, NOVEMBER 6, 2021

HUMILITY

1. HUMILITY HELPS US FOCUS ON UNITY.
- God is glorified when we are unified.
- When there is a lack of unity - there also is a lack of joy, comfort, and encouragement.
- Unity is absolutely essential to the body of Christ. The quickest way to kill a body part is to cut it off from the body.

2. HUMILITY HELPS US FOCUS ON OUR RESPONSIBILITY.
- Greater humility always leads us to greater responsibility.
- Service that does not cost you something will not accomplish anything.

3. HUMILITY HELPS US FOCUS ON ETERNITY.
- When we reflect on eternity, we are reminded that we are leaving a legacy.
- Jesus left a legacy of love and sacrifice.
- What will be your legacy?

PHILIPPIANS 2

1 So if there is any encouragement in Christ, any comfort from love, any participation in the Spirit, any affection and sympathy, 2 complete my joy by being of the same mind, having the same love, being in full accord and of one mind. 3 Do nothing from selfish ambition or conceit, but in humility count others more significant than yourselves. 4 Let each of you look not only to his own interests, but also to the interests of others. 5 Have this mind among yourselves, which is yours in Christ Jesus, 6 who, though he was in the form of God, did not count equality with God a thing to be grasped, 7 but emptied himself, by taking the form of a servant, being born in the likeness of men. 8 And being found in human form, he humbled himself by becoming obedient to the point of death, even death on a cross. 9 Therefore God has highly exalted him and bestowed on him the name that is above every name, 10 so that at the name of Jesus every knee should bow, in heaven and on earth and under the earth, 11 and every tongue confess that Jesus Christ is Lord, to the glory of God the Father.

Rk	Date	Opponent	Result	Passing Cmp	Att	Pct	Yds	TD	Rushing Att	Yds	Avg	TD	Total Offense Plays	Yds	Avg	First Downs Pass	Rush	Pen	Tot	Penalties No.	Yds	Turnovers Fum	Int	Tot
9	11/6/21	Missouri	W (43-6)	20	30	66.7	337	3	33	168	5.1	2	63	505	8	17	7	1	25	4	35	0	1	1

SANFORD STADIUM

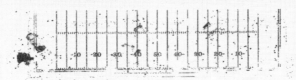

W 43-6
GAME TIME: 12:00 P.M. EST
GAME ATTENDANCE: 92,746

CHAPTER 10
BELIEVE

KNOXVILLE, TN
NOVEMBER 13, 2021

4 But God, being rich in mercy, because of the great love with which he loved us,5 even when we were dead in our trespasses, made us alive together with Christ—by grace you have been saved— 6 and raised us up with him and seated us with him in the heavenly places in Christ Jesus, 7 so that in the coming ages he might show the immeasurable riches of his grace in kindness toward us in Christ Jesus. 8 For by grace you have been saved through faith. And this is not your own doing; it is the gift of God, 9 not a result of works, so that no one may boast. 10 For we are his workmanship created in Christ Jesus for good works, which God prepared beforehand, that we should walk in them.
Ephesians 2:4-10

The older I get the more I appreciate those who started from nothing and were able to accomplish something. A couple of years ago, I came across an article that highlighted three businesses that started from nothing. In 1923, Walt Disney founded the first Disney studio. In 1976, Steve Jobs founded Apple. In 1994, Jeff Bezos founded Amazon.com. Think for a second, do you know what Disney, Apple, and Amazon have in common? What those three companies have in common is that they all started in a garage. Today, 42 cents of every dollar that is spent on the internet goes through Amazon, but it was started in a garage. Those companies have had so much success and made so much money, but it all started because someone believed.

If you go back and watch any interview about their origin stories and their humble beginnings, what you will hear is that those men never stopped believing. You will hear that everyone thought they were crazy. You will hear how no one understood why they worked so hard. You will hear that plenty of people had told them to quit, or that it wouldn't work out and that it wasn't worth it. People told them to do something different. They told them their dream could never come true. But they never stopped believing. Many times, we hear some of the same things about the team.

"Do y'all really practice that hard?"

"Do you guys really watch all of that film?"

"Y'all really gonna play a game, fly home, and be back at the football complex Sunday to work out?"

People don't believe in what we do, but because we believe, we are willing to put in the work.

When we think about the world there are some wonderful and powerful forces that can be experienced. There is the power of wind that can turn into a hurricane or a tornado and tear apart a town. There is the power of water that could flood an entire city. There is even the power of fire that can burn down a city. But I want to submit to you that belief has a different kind of power. When we believe, we don't simply see things torn down. When we believe we don't simply see things torn apart. When we believe, we have the ability to build something great for God. Belief has the ability to create something great. Belief has the ability to leave something behind that will always be remembered. Belief is like the wind. You can't see it, but you can feel it. You can't see the wind, but you can see its impact. Can you tangibly see faith or belief? No, but you can see its impact. There is not a person living today that does not operate by faith or belief. Now some of us might be a little more religious than others, but all of us operate based upon belief or faith. Male or female, young or old, rich or poor, black or white — all of us live out our faith.

Think about the last chair in which you sat. Before you sat down, did you check your seat? When you got home from work, did you check to see if the TV was plugged in, or did you just hit the remote? Did you check and see if the remote had batteries, or did you just hit the button? Since we all have faith, the text is not simply encouraging us to believe, but it is encouraging us to place belief in the right place. Has anybody ever seen a basketball player make a great steal, but in the heat of the moment, he got turned around so that he was dribbling toward the opposite basket? The player makes a great play, but he is about to score for the other team, and as the player is running to the wrong hoop, thankfully, one of his teammates catches his attention before he scores for the other team.

Essentially that is what our passage is doing for us this morning. God doesn't want us to put our faith in the wrong place. This past week, I had a member of our church come to me crying. She and her husband sold their house, and they wanted to give some money to the church from the sale. Somehow, there was an issue where the money ended up being sent somewhere else. She thought she was sending it to our church, but because of an error, we didn't receive it. Paul is writing to a group that misunderstood the power of believing. They have made great plays, but they are trying to put the ball in the wrong hoop. They are about to put points on the board for the other team. So that passage tells us there are specific places to put our belief. It gives us three specific places to put our trust, and the first thing we see is that we are encouraged to believe in God's grace.

1. Believing in God's Grace

8 For by grace you have been saved through faith. And this is not your own doing; it is the gift of God,

A couple of years ago, I was on the Oprah Winfrey show. True story. When I went to Morehouse I wasn't on an athletic scholarship, but I received some academic aid from a special fund. At the time, I didn't know it, but the money that helped me pay for school was given by Oprah. Back in 2011, as she was ending her historic run of a daytime talk show, they did a huge celebration at the United Center in Chicago, where the Bulls play. The show was filled with surprises, including a visit from a host of past guests. There were celebrities everywhere like Beyonce, Tom Hanks, Halle Berry, Tyler Perry, Tom Cruise, and the list goes on and on. Well, to surprise Ms. Winfrey they wanted to bring some guys on stage whom she had helped make it through college. There were 300 guys who were in attendance, but only about 15 to 20 of us got to go on stage. Now you know ya' boy was on stage for sure! I mean, I knew my momma was watching, and she wanted to see me! Now because the select students were going to be onstage, we got the VIP treatment. I met everyone I mentioned. I met Tom Cruise, and he is about the size of Logan Johnson. Beyonce was of average height. Halle Berry really was gorgeous.

Now don't miss this. Because I responded the right way, I got to experience meeting celebrities. I got to fly to Chicago. I got to stay at the 5-star hotel. I got to be on stage as well. And you know what? It was all grace. It wasn't my GPA that got me there. It wasn't my degree that got me there. It wasn't my charm and wit. I was there because of a gracious invitation.

Now when I received the scholarship, I was broke. I didn't have anything. I was able to get a partial student loan, but the school was so expensive that my loans didn't even cover all my tuition. Because I couldn't come up with the tuition, I was about to be kicked out of school, and what she gave to the school saved me. What she gave to the school was credited to my account. I didn't have anything to put on the account, but she graciously gave, and what she gave was put on my account. The Bible says we were dead in our sins until Jesus made us alive. We were spiritually bankrupt until Jesus stepped in, and we had to receive the invitation. When I got the invitation to go to the show, it was an invitation that I ignored until one of my best friends told me about it. In that same way, God's grace is an invitation that we don't have to earn, but it is one that we have to respond to.

In the text, God does not begin with guilt. He begins with GRACE! Grace should be a great motivator because it reminds us of all that God has done. When I got to Chicago, Ms. Winfrey's attitude wasn't one where she made us feel guilty for what she had done, but she gave us grace. Since we haven't been saved by our good works, we can't be lost by our bad works.

Believe in God's grace.

2. Believing in God's Gift

8 For by grace you have been saved through faith. And this is not your own doing; it is the gift of God, 9 not a result of works, so that no one may boast.

Think for a second – what is the greatest gift you have been given? Was it a car? Was it your scholarship? Was it some money? Was it an opportunity? I want to submit to you that a car is a good gift, but not the greatest gift. Money is a good gift, but not the greatest gift. In time, you can work to get your own car. In time, you can work and get your own money. In time, you can work and get more opportunities, but I want to submit to you that the greatest gift that God gives us is something we could never get ourselves. Now it's cool if you give me something sooner than I could have gotten it myself, but the real blessing is when you get something that you could have never gotten on your own. Something that you could have never gotten from anyone else. The greatest gift we receive is from Jesus because He gives us what we would not get on our own.

Let me submit to you that the possession of our faith will never be as important as the object of our faith.

The possession of faith will never be as important as the object of faith.

One of my favorite stories of revealing authentic belief is the story of Charles Blondin, the French tightrope walker. On June 30, 1859, he did his most famous act when he became the first person to cross a tightrope stretched across the mighty Niagara Falls. The tightrope was more than a quarter mile long, suspended 160 feet above the Falls. He walked across several times, each time in a different way: once on stilts, once on a bike, and once blindfolded! A large crowd gathered to watch with each feat bringing louder applause. At a different performance, the crowd ooooh-ed and ahhhh-ed as Blondin carefully walked across, taking one dangerous step after another, pushing a wheelbarrow holding a huge sack of potatoes.

Then at one point, he asked the crowd, "Do you believe I can carry a person across in this wheelbarrow?"

The crowd enthusiastically yelled, "Yes! Yes! We believe! You are the greatest tightrope walker in the world. We believe!"

Okay," said Blondin, "who wants to get into the wheelbarrow?"

No response. Crickets. They said they believed, but no one was willing to get into the wheelbarrow.

Believe in God's gift.

3. Believing in God's Game Plan

¹⁰For we are his workmanship, created in Christ Jesus for good

works, which God prepared beforehand, that we should walk in them.

I love my kids, and I am thankful for them. But if I'm honest, over the holidays, it can be kind of tough to enjoy their numerous art projects. As the season approaches, they bring home a variety of art for me to critique and praise. As the creativity mounts, the truth of the matter is that I become "art fatigued". Considering this, let's look closer at verse 10.

Verse 10 is super important because it communicates that we are a work of art, not the kind of art that my kids bring home, but the kind of work that God will bring home to be in heaven with Him. We are God'swork of art. We are God's workmanship created in Christ Jesus to do good works. What does that mean? That means that you are not here by accident! And you are the way you are by design.

Just like Coach Monken has designed a game plan. Just like Coach Lanning has designed a game plan. Just like Coach Smart has designed a game plan. God has a game plan for you, and He has called you to believe in that plan. God's plan is not just to bless you, but to make you a blessing. God's plan is that you be used, but we can't be used until we are willing to be humble. God's plan is that you know Him and that you help others know Him.

are willing to be humble. God's plan is that you know Him and that you help others know Him.

Believe in God's grace.

Believe in God's gift.

Believe in God's game plan.

Believe.

Want to know more about a relationship with God?

Scan here to find out how you can know God personally.

DEVOTIONAL
KNOXVILLE, TN
SATURDAY, NOVEMBER 13, 2021

BELIEVE

1. BELIEVING IN GOD'S GRACE
- God does not begin with guilt. He begins with GRACE!
- Grace should be a great motivator, because it reminds us of all that God has done!
- Since we have not been saved by our good works, we can not be lost by our bad works.

2. BELIEVING IN GOD'S GIFT
- We are saved by grace alone, through faith alone, in Christ alone.
- The possession of our faith will never be as important as the object of our faith.

3. BELIEVING IN GOD'S GAME PLAN
- We are not saved by our works, but we are saved to work.
- Being God's "workmanship" is not achieved by good works, but it results in good works.
- The same loving Father who chose us, called us, and saved us has also marked out a wonderful plan for us!
- Sin worked against us. Christ worked for us, and the Holy Spirit wants to work in us.

EPHESIANS 2

4 But God, being rich in mercy, because of the great love with which he loved us, 5 even when we were dead in our trespasses, made us alive together with Christ—by grace you have been saved—6 and raised us up with him and seated us with him in the heavenly places in Christ Jesus, 7 so that in the coming ages he might show the immeasurable riches of his grace in kindness toward us in Christ Jesus. 8 For by grace you have been saved through faith. And this is not your own doing; it is the gift of God, 9 not a result of works, so that no one may boast. 10 For we are his workmanship, created in Christ Jesus for good works, which God prepared beforehand, that we should walk in them.

W 41-17

GAME TIME: 3:30 P.M. EST
GAME ATTENDANCE: 100,074

Rk	Date	Opponent	Result	Passing					Rushing				Total Offense			First Downs				Penalties		Turnovers		
				Cmp	Att	Pct	Yds	TD	Att	Yds	Avg	TD	Plays	Yds	Avg	Pass	Rush	Pen	Tot	No.	Yds	Fum	Int	Tot
10	11/13/21 @ Tennessee		W (41-17)	17	29	58.6	213	1	41	274	6.7	4	70	487	7	12	14	0	26	5	55	0	0	0

NEYLAND STADIUM

CHAPTER 11
MISTAKES: THE DANGER OF DRIFTING

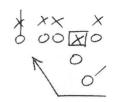

ATHENS, GA
NOVEMBER 20, 2021

1 Therefore we must pay much closer attention to what we have heard, lest we drift away from it. 2 For since the message declared by angels proved to be reliable, and every transgression or disobedience received a just retribution, 3 how shall we escape if we neglect such a great salvation? It was declared at first by the Lord, and it was attested to us by those who heard, 4 while God also bore witness by signs and wonders and various miracles and by gifts of the Holy Spirit distributed according to his will.
Hebrews 2:1-4

One of the worst days I have had as a chaplain came back in 2007. We took a group of athletes up to the Broad River in Danielsville. It was an event for all athletes to help build community and have some fun, so we all bused up to the Broad River. Now during that time, I was big T. Settles. I tell people I was 305 lbs., but in truth, it was more like 345 lbs. Now when we went up there, they told me it would be fun. They said you just get in the tube, and you just drift down the river. You don't have to row at all; you can just simply relax and drift. That's what they told me.

What they didn't tell me was how hard it would be to get into the tube when you are weighing in at 345 pounds. What they didn't tell me was there were plenty of snakes in the water. What they didn't tell me was that because the water was low, you could get stuck if you were heavy. They'll have to get you out of the tube and figure out how to get back inside. Again, all they told me was that it would be fun, and all I I needed to do was drift.

Here is the truth – in life, drifting might sound good, but some things come along with drifting that we usually don't hear about. As we get ready for our last home game tomorrow, I want to encourage us not to drift. We don't need to drift in the game tomorrow, but also, we don't need to drift in any area of our lives. Notice I didn't say "you". I intentionally said "us". The way life is set up, drifting is not just an easy thing. It's a probable thing. We are likely and prone to drift.

Drifting requires only one thing. It only requires that you stop making an effort. All you have to do is stop taking a situation seriously. All it means is that you are trying less than before, and that is the major point that this passage is communicating. Hear me clearly: the scripture is addressing a group of really good people. This is not a group of criminals. This is not a bunch of murderers and killers. This passage is written to the good guys — a group of people who had faithfully followed Jesus in the past, a group of people who were very similar to the group of people reading this book right now. This is the group that began to drift away from the Lord.

The act of drifting is a subtle and gradual process. The spiritual impact of drifting is not sudden or spectacular. The drift is usually gentle and subtle.

In the Book of Hebrews, there is a community of Christians living in a time of trials. That community is not so different from yours and mine. Like us, they had struggles. Like us, they faced issues. Like us, they had questions about God. Like us, they wrestled with what it really looked like to live out their faith, and like us, they had the tendency to drift away from the Lord.

When we take the time to wrestle with whether or not we are drifting, it is not uncommon to realize that it is unintentional. We don't plan it, but because life is busy and chaotic, it just sort of happens. We are slowly pulled away, swayed by other things that we allow the less important to become something of primary importance. We wake up one day and realize things seem different. We find ourselves in a place we'd never intended to be. A spiritual drift can happen for many different reasons. Sometimes, it's because of busyness. Sometimes, it's because we experienced hurt. It occurs sometimes in good seasons of life and other times in rough ones. By definition, "to drift" means "a continuous slow movement from one place to another". It doesn't happen quickly, and it can be hard to identify that it is occurring.

To help you out, I wanted to identify some signs of drifting that you may be experiencing. Think about your game in Sanford. Are you as passionate as you used to be? Think about that first game where you expected to play. You are not as focused as you used to be. You are not as hungry as you used to be. How excited were you the night you moved into the spacious ECV student housing? Think about the night before your first start. Are you as excited today as you were then? Are you as excited about playing Charleston Southern as you were Clemson? For those who are not on the football team, are you as excited about the career as you were when you first began the job? Are you as excited about your marriage as you used to be? Are you as thankful for your children and your family as you used to be?

If you can identify with any of those things I just mentioned, there is encouragement for you in the text. Because of God's love for us and because of God's plan for us, God blessed us with a passage that highlights the dangers of drifting. He also provides an antidote to the condition as well. The first thing we see is a reminder that we need an anchor.

1. The Reminder That We Need an Anchor (v.1)

2:1 Therefore we must pay much closer attention to what we have heard, lest we drift away from it.

Verse 1 starts with "Therefore," which should cause us to reflect on what immediately came before it. The author of Hebrews uses the word *therefore* because we need to pay close attention to it. It's so easy to forget. It's so easy to lose sight. It's so easy to let it slip our minds. We need to pay attention, not to people's opinions, as we learned from last week's lesson on Believing. The passage reminds us that we need to pay close attention to what we believe. When we fail to pay close attention to Jesus. we end up drifting, and the consequences of drifting are usually departing from God's will, missing God's best for our lives, and grieving the heart of God. The text tells us that the key to not drifting is to pay close attention to what we have heard about Jesus.

If paying close attention to Jesus keeps us from drifting, then we can conclude that Christ is the anchor in the life of a Christian.

How do we drift? When we wake up early enough to make it to class, but we don't wake up early enough to make time for prayer and devotions.

How do we drift? When we are concerned about pleasing man rather than God.

How do we drift? When we are offended by things that bother us, but we look past things that offend God.

How do we drift? We drift when life becomes about us and not about the Lord.

When you read the text, the author did not fear them making a huge quick U-turn. He is more concerned about the slow and steady drift that takes place when you are not paying attention to Jesus. When we drift, we always miss God's best. Let's say someone is headed home for Thanksgiving, and he calls his mom and tells her, "I'm headed home. I will be there in 1.5 hours." And Momma says, "Ok, baby. I'm going to cook your favorite meal. You don't need to stop and eat on the road. I will have your favorite meal ready for you when you get home." On the drive home, there will be a lot of temptation to stop, but Mom has been preparing something for you that is better for you. The same is true in our relationship with God. Yes, we will be tempted to drift. We will be tempted to compromise. We will be tempted to cut corners. But we want to stay focused on Christ so that we can receive God's best. We need an anchor because it is so easy to drift. And when we drift, we miss God's best.

First, we see we need an anchor. But why?

2. The Reason Why We Need an Anchor (vv.2-3)

2 For since the message declared by angels proved to be reliable, and every transgression or disobedience received a just retribution, 3 how shall we escape if we neglect such a great salvation? It was declared at first by the Lord, and it was attested to us by those who heard,

The passage reminds us of the payment made for our salvation. Our salvation is a "great salvation," purchased at a great price. It brings with it great promises and great blessings, and it leads to a great inheritance in glory. Salvation is far too great to neglect it! Some might be wondering how we can neglect it. Verse 3 declares, "How shall we escape if we neglect such a great salvation?"

When we read verse 3, it is not wrong to ask the question, what is so great about salvation? The answer is that we know salvation is great because of its essence and its origin. Let's focus on the essence of salvation first. Salvation is great because it is the one thing that every person needs more than anything else. I love verse 3 because it allows us to see the significance of salvation by adding the word escape. It says, "How shall we escape...?" An escape points to a situation of great peril. You don't need to be saved unless you are in grave danger of perishing. Salvation does not mean that Jesus helps you fulfill your dreams. Salvation is not about Jesus simply improving your marriage or giving you peace and joy. Will a relationship with God improve your life? Of course.

But God's salvation isn't the icing on the cake of your successful and happy life.

Salvation is about Jesus rescuing you from the wrath to come, and since every person is in imminent danger of facing that wrath, salvation is every person's greatest need!

Salvation is great not only because of its essence but also because of its origin. Salvation is great because it comes to us from none other than the Lord himself. Salvation is far too good to come from any place other than God. Every religion will tell you about works that are required to get to God. You have to reach Nirvana. You have to go on a pilgrimage, but the Gospel reminds us that God comes to us. Amen.

First, we have a reminder that we need an anchor. Secondly, we have the reason why we need an anchor.

And thirdly, we have the results of having an anchor.

3. The Results of Having an Anchor (v. 4)

4 while God also bore witness by signs and wonders and various miracles and by gifts of the Holy Spirit distributed according to his will.

God doesn't simply tell us that we need an anchor, but the text reminds us of the testimony of men and women who were anchored. In the Bible, those who were anchored accomplished some great things, and their testimonies were dynamic. Their testimonies included "Signs." Signs helped others believe in God. It included "Wonders," which helped people be in awe of God, and it included "Miracles," which showed others the power of God beyond human ability, and "Gifts of the Holy Spirit," which help us serve.

All four — signs, wonders, miracles, and gifts, were all mighty demonstrations of God's presence in the lives of His people. Now when we read this section, it is very easy for us to assume that we need to pursue signs, wonders, miracles, and works of the Spirit so that the Gospel will be confirmed today. But rather than pursuing those things, may we give our lives pursuing Jesus.

There is a true story that was told by a pastor by the name of Billy Norris. Norris shares the story of two young men who were fishing. They had gone to this particular fishing hole many times before, and since they had been there often, they got comfortable. This was not just some ordinary finishing hole, as they were fishing on a river that was connected to a dam. The boys knew that the dam was scheduled to release some water later in the day, but they figured they would catch a couple of fish and be done well before the water was released. Well, the boys were out fishing for several hours, and the entire time they were out on the water, they were concentrating on catching fish. They were enjoying the beautiful day. They were telling stories, and they were loving life. Unfortunately, they were so focused on the fish that they didn't realize they were drifting dangerously close to the dam. The sirens begin to go off to warn that water was about to be released. They began trying to paddle in the opposite direction of the current, but the current was so powerful that they couldn't do anything to keep the boat from going over the ledge. And when the boat went over the ledge, it crashed against the rocks and broke apart. The boys were caught in the undercurrent, and they never came to the surface. After days of searching, the divers finally found one of the bodies. And then several days later, they found the second body. The story I just shared is true, and as a father, it breaks my heart to hear that story because I have boys who I love more than anything. The story also breaks my heart as a pastor because many of us are drifting in countless areas of our lives.

Notice I didn't say "you". Again, I intentionally said "us"!

Application:

We should not neglect the relationship we have with the Lord. It's wonderful to fall in love and get married. I highly recommend the experience, but marriage is a relationship, and relationships take time and effort to maintain. I don't care how deeply you were in love when you got married; if you neglect your marriage and devote your attention to other things, your marriage will suffer. Salvation is much greater than marriage, and it takes even more effort.

Don't let it drift!

Don't neglect it!

Don't get distracted with other things, even with good things!

Pay close attention to what you have heard. How can you pay close attention to what Jesus has said if you are not in the Word? If you are not in church? If you are not in a small group? If you are not studying on your own?

Pray that the Lord keeps you from temptation.

GAME ELEVEN
DEVOTIONAL CARD

PRE-GAME CHAPEL
ATHENS, GA
SATURDAY, NOVEMBER 20, 2021

MISTAKES: THE DANGER OF DRIFTING

1. THE REMINDER THAT WE NEED AN ANCHOR
- Jesus is not only the savior of our souls, but also the anchor of our lives.
  The key to not drifting is paying close attention.
- When we drift, we always miss God's best for our lives.

2. THE REASON WHY WE NEED AN ANCHOR
- We need an anchor because we are all prone to drift.
- The Gospel is a reminder of the good news and the bad news. The bad news is we are more sinful than we would like to admit. The good news is we are more loved than we can ever imagine.
- Scripture certainly highlights the issue of sin, but most importantly, the antidote to it.

3. THE RESULTS OF HAVING AN ANCHOR
- Signs, wonders, miracles and gifts were a demonstration of God working in and through the lives of believers.
- How is God working in your life? How is God working through your life?

HEBREWS 2

1 Therefore we must pay much closer attention to what we have heard, lest we drift away from it. 2 For since the message declared by angels proved to be reliable, and every transgression or disobedience received a just retribution, 3 how shall we escape if we neglect such a great salvation? It was declared at first by the Lord, and it was attested to us by those who heard, 4 while God also bore witness by signs and wonders and various miracles and by gifts of the Holy Spirit distributed according to his will.

W 56-7

GAME TIME: 12:00 P.M. EST
GAME ATTENDANCE: 92,746

Rk	Date	Opponent	Result	Passing					Rushing				Total Offense			First Downs				Penalties		Turnovers		
				Cmp	Att	Pct	Yds	TD	Att	Yds	Avg	TD	Plays	Yds	Avg	Pass	Rush	Pen	Tot	No.	Yds	Fum	Int	Tot
11	11/20/21	Charleston Southern	W (56-7)	20	37	54.1	255	4	32	233	7.3	4	69	488	7.1	12	9	1	22	2	25	1	2	3

SANFORD STADIUM

CHAPTER 12
ACCOUNTABILITY

ATLANTA, GA
NOVEMBER 27, 2021

10 On their return the apostles told him all that they had done. And he took them and withdrew apart to a town called Bethsaida. 11 When the crowds learned it, they followed him, and he welcomed them and spoke to them of the kingdom of God and cured those who had need of healing. 12 Now the day began to wear away, and the twelve came and said to him, "Send the crowd away to go into the surrounding villages and countryside to find lodging and get provisions, for we are here in a desolate place." 13 But he said to them, "You give them something to eat." They said, "We have no more than five loaves and two fish—unless we are to go and buy food for all these people." 14 For there were about five thousand men. And he said to his disciples, "Have them sit down in groups of about fifty each." 15 And they did so, and had them all sit down. 16 And taking the five loaves and the two fish, he looked up to heaven and said a blessing over them. Then he broke the loaves and gave them to the disciples to set before the crowd. 17 And they all ate and were satisfied. And what was left over was picked up, twelve baskets of broken pieces. 18 Now it happened that as he was praying alone, the disciples were with him. And he asked them, "Who do the crowds say that I am?" 19 And they answered, "John the Baptist. But others say, Elijah, and others, that one of the prophets of old has risen." 20 Then he said to them, "But who do you say that I am?" And Peter answered, "The Christ of God."
Luke 9:10 -20

It has been said that in life, the right things must be placed in the right hands to see certain results. A basketball in my hands is worth about $15. But a basketball in Michael Jordan's hands can be turned into 6 championships. A baseball bat in my hands is worth about $20. But a baseball in Hank Aaron's hands is worth a home run title. A tennis racket is useless in my hand, but a tennis racket in Serena William's hand can become a Wimbledon championship. A rod in my hands will keep away a wild animal, but a rod in Moses' hands could part a mighty sea. A slingshot in my hands is a kid's toy, but a slingshot in David's hand is a powerful weapon. Two fish and 5 loaves of bread in my hand are a couple of fish sandwiches. Two fish and 5 loaves of bread in God's hands will feed thousands. As you see, things in life can be changed or transformed depending upon whose hands they are placed in!

I believe that's what our passage is essentially communicating. We see miracles when we put the right things in the hands of God. There is not an area of your life that you cannot entrust to God. Brothers and sisters, I want you to know that God invites us to trust Him in every area of life when we place the right things in His hands. We will see a miracle. We will see God bless it. And we will see God make us a blessing! Go with me to verse 11 again...

1. The Problem

11 When the crowds learned it, they followed him, and he welcomed them and spoke to them of the kingdom of God and cured those who had need of healing. 12 Now the day began to wear away, and the twelve came and said to him, "Send the crowd away to go into the surrounding villages and countryside to find lodging and get provisions, for we are here in a desolate place." 13 But he said to them, "You give them something to eat." They said, "We have no more than five loaves and two fish—unless we are to go and buy food for all these people."

At this point in the text, Jesus had been preaching and teaching, and the crowds got larger the more that he taught. The preaching of Jesus was so powerful that people not only came to hear from him. But they would not leave because they did not want to miss an opportunity to receive something from him. This was creating a huge problem. Here you have thousands of people who have come to hear from Jesus, and they're refusing to leave. And while they had been receiving some spiritual food from the sermon, it was time for some physical food for their bodies.

The people hadn't planned to follow Jesus, and so there was nothing to eat.

To appreciate what is taking place in the text, we must understand that they lived in a day and time without fast food. There was no Chick-fil-A. There was no McDonalds. There wasn't a Wendy's. They couldn't order a pizza, and here they are at a church service with 5,000 plus hungry people. It's Sunday, so Chick-fil-A is closed anyway. But not only CFA, but so are the other options like McDonald's, Wendy's, Raisin' Canes, and Chipotle, all closed.

So, this was a real problem. But it's a problem that presents us with an opportunity to consider how we respond to problems in our lives. Pause and just think for a second. How do you respond when there is a problem, not just in your life, but also in the lives of others?

From reading the text, we clearly see that there are two very different responses to the problem they faced. The disciples responded to the problem by saying, "Send them away" (v.12). They wanted to ignore the problem. They wanted to dismiss the problem. They didn't want to deal with the problem. They just wanted to move on. They didn't want to really deal with the problem. They wanted to get rid of the problem by sending away the problem by washing their hands of the issue rather than doing something to address the issue.

The disciples wanted to deal with the problem by sending the people away, but Jesus responded to the problem by saying, "Sit them down." Hearing Jesus say, "Sit them down," should challenge us that when we see a need, we should look to meet those needs! Jesus is teaching us that when you see a problem, you own it! If you see a need, then you should do everything by the power of God to meet that need.

Last Sunday, we did an outreach at the church I have the privilege of serving as pastor at, Calvary Bible Church. We got together with DFCS and the schools close to the church, and we gave food boxes to folks in need. The church paid for everything, but we asked the families of our church to break up into groups so that we could do the disbursement together. Now it was nice to do that for Thanksgiving. I believe in my heart we should do more than give on Thanksgiving. My son asked me why we were giving out the turkeys, and I responded to him that it's not enough for us to be ok, but we want others to have everything that they need. Whenever we see a need, we need to speak to that need rather than trying to ignore a need.

In the text, Jesus is reminding us that we don't simply preach to people. We are also called to serve people. Let me ask you a question as you read this chapter. Have you ever considered that maybe God is revealing problems around you? Maybe God is revealing needs around you so that you can be used to address those problems and serve those needs. When you see a need in your life or in the lives of others, do you do everything you can to meet that need? Do you trust that God will give you what you need to meet those needs? Or do you respond like the disciples and try to go with the path of least resistance by simply sending it away? As we follow Jesus with our lives, I believe we should see these as precious opportunities to bless people rather than ignoring the needs of others and dismissing the needs of others. We have been blessed to be a blessing.

First, we see the problem.

Next, we see the provision.

2. The Provision (vv. 13-17)

15 And they did so, and had them all sit down. 16 And taking the five loaves and the two fish, he looked up to heaven and said a blessing over them. Then he broke the loaves and gave them to the disciples to set before the crowd.

God provided all they needed but in ways that were unexpected. Earlier in the book, I told you a story about how I ended up moving to Athens and doing ministry. As a refresher, before I was in Athens, I was on staff at a large church in Atlanta. I got a call from this crazy guy named Chappy. He had posted my job online. A guy I went to seminary with had applied for the position and didn't get it. They declined him, and then they asked him if he knew of anyone who would be a good candidate. He gave them my number, and the rest is history. What I didn't tell you is how Casey and I got close.

Casey and I met in seminary. Casey was an older guy, and he had been out of school for a while. He didn't understand how to use Microsoft Word, and he was unfamiliar with how to properly cite his papers. Casey was struggling, and when I saw his struggle, I felt the need to help. I didn't just ignore his struggle. I was willing to serve and assist. Fast forward to years later, the guy who I helped in the computer lab was the same guy who recommended me for this dream job.

In the text, you have a problem, but you also have an unexpected provision from a little boy. I love reading this passage because it is a reminder that you don't have to wait until you are old to serve God. You don't have to live in a way where you waste your best years living in the world. And then, eventually, you give God your leftovers. While I love Thanksgiving, I can't stand leftovers. Growing up, we didn't just do leftovers during Thanksgiving. Man, we would do leftovers Sunday through Wednesday. Even now, my parents would do leftovers so much that I'm still traumatized. Even this morning, after Thanksgiving, I want something fresh. I don't want the leftovers.

God doesn't want your leftovers, either. In God's economy, young people, even people who the world would say don't have much to offer, can make a significant impact on God's kingdom. Satan wants us to believe the lie that service in God's kingdom is reserved for the old folks. It's reserved for the perfect folks. That it's reserved for the seminary folks. Satan wants us to believe the lie that making an impact for Christ is something that we will get to later. Something that we will get to after we have our fun...after we enjoy our youth. But hear me clearly — that is a lie! When we read the scriptures, we see a ton of young people who did great things for God! You see a young David who killed a lion and a bear and slayed Goliath! You see a young Joshua who faithfully leads the nation! You see a young Samuel who served the Lord. You have a young man named Timothy who was a great leader in the church.

Catch the progression. The little boy had to give what he had. He had to surrender it before God could use it. If we are honest, a lot of us don't see God using us in areas of our lives because we won't surrender it.

The little boy went beyond allowing Jesus to look at the lunch. The little boy didn't say, *Jesus, you can look at my lunch on Friday night at chapel.* He didn't say *you can hold my lunch 5-10 minutes a day a couple of times a week.* He didn't say *I'll lend you my lunch when I get a title or a certain position in the church.* He didn't say *I will give you my lunch if you give me the things I have prayed for.* He gave it all. He fully surrendered it! And Jesus received it and blessed it.

In the text, we see the problem – 5,000 people with no food to eat.

Then, we see the provision – a sack lunch from a little boy.

And lastly, we see a profound picture.

3. The Picture

17 And they all ate and were satisfied. And what was left over was picked up, twelve baskets of broken pieces. 18 Now it happened that as he was praying alone, the disciples were with him. And he asked them, "Who do the crowds say that I am?" 19 And they answered, "John the Baptist. But others say, Elijah, and others, that one of the prophets of old has risen." 20 Then he said to them, "But who do you say that I am?" And Peter answered, "The Christ of God."

Here is what we see in the passage. The Lord looked up to heaven, the source of our daily bread. He gave thanks and blessed the food, and then He multiplied the few loaves and fishes. In the text, Jesus was the "producer," and His disciples were the "distributors." And the amazing thing is everybody was served and satisfied. That's what happens when we surrender to the Lord. Everyone is served. Everyone is satisfied. And the way God does it, there is even a leftover blessing, so we are reminded of God's grace.

The disciples wanted to send them away, but Jesus worked in such a gracious and mighty way that there were twelve baskets left over. Twelve testimonies to speak to the faithfulness of God. Twelve testimonies that with God, all things are possible. Twelve examples of

how Jesus takes good care of His servants. Please understand that this miracle was more than an act of mercy
for hungry people, though that was important. It was also a sign of our Lord's messiahship and an illustration of God's gracious provision for man's salvation.

Later on in the narrative, Jesus preached a sermon on "the bread of life" and urged the people to receive Him just as they had received the bread. But the people were more interested in their stomachs than their souls. They completely missed the spiritual impact of the miracle. Their desire was to make Jesus a King so He could give them bread for the rest of their lives. But Jesus was more interested in giving them eternal life.

This is a powerful picture for us because God wants you to place your life in his hands the very same way that the little boy placed his lunch in His hands. Beyond just at the moment of salvation, God wants you to place your life in his hands on a daily basis. God wants you to fully trust Him in every area of your life. Think about the text. It took a lot of trust for that young boy to place what he had in the hands of Jesus. And that is exactly what God wants you to do with your life. The Christian life is a journey where we are placing our lives in God's hands. The Christian life flourishes when we allow our gifts, what God has placed in our lives, to be a blessing to others, not so that we can get more credit, but so that God can receive the glory!

Jesus ends the section with a question, "Who do men say that I am?" Earlier in the chapter, Herod had asked the question "Who is this man?" For some, Jesus is no different than a rabbit's foot. Now Jesus is asking the question, "Who do men say that I am? The question concerning who Jesus is is a question that we must answer. Some say he was simply a wise teacher and operated as if Jesus was a sage whom they could consult for good advice. Others say that he was a deeply religious man who spoke with authority but did not possess divinity. Some say he is a lunatic, a crazy man with crazy sayings that make no sense. Some say he is a liar making promises that he could not possibly keep. But others have recognized him as Lord.

So let me ask you that question as you read this devotional:

Who do you say that He is?

I'm not asking about your parents or your friends or even your pastor, but who do you say that he is? Have you come to the place in your life where you have received Christ as your Lord and Savior? Are you responding to the problems in your life in light of your relationship with the Lord?

God will never ask you to give what you don't have. God only asked you to give back what he has already given to you.

Your life is a gift from God, and the best thing you can do is to give it back.

Your time is a gift from God, and the best thing you can do is give it back.

Your talent is a gift from God, and the best thing you can do is give it back.

Your treasure or your resources are all gifts from God, and the best thing you can do with it is to give it back.

GAME TWELVE
DEVOTIONAL CARD

PRE-GAME CHAPEL
ATLANTA, GA
SATURDAY, NOVEMBER 27, 2021

ACCOUNTABILITY

1. THE PROBLEM - NO FOOD, OR MONEY TO BUY IT
- There were thousands of people with nothing to eat.
- How do you respond to the problems in your life?
- The disciples wanted to dismiss the problem rather than using what God provided to deal with the problem.

2. THE PROVISION - A SACK LUNCH FROM A LITTLE BOY
- God provided all that they needed - but in ways that were unexpected.
- The young man in the story reminds us that we don't have to wait until we are old to serve God.
- Rather than making an excuse, the boy made a sacrifice. We want to give God our best, not just the leftovers.

3. THE PICTURE - A LIFE SURRENDERED TO GOD
- We should read the story and ask ourselves the question: "Am I willing to trust God with my life?"
- We must always remember that God doesn't simply want to bless us .... God wants to make us a blessing to others.

LUKE 9

10 On their return the apostles told him all that they had done. And he took them and withdrew apart to a town called Bethsaida. 11 When the crowds learned it, they followed him, and he welcomed them and spoke to them of the kingdom of God and cured those who had need of healing. 12 Now the day began to wear away, and the twelve came and said to him, "Send the crowd away to go into the surrounding villages and countryside to find lodging and get provisions, for we are here in a desolate place." 13.But he said to them, "You give them something to eat." They said, "We have no more than five loaves and two fish—unless we are to go and buy food for all these people." 14 For there were about five thousand men. And he said to his disciples, "Have them sit down in groups of about fifty each."15 And they did so, and had them all sit down. 16 And taking the five loaves and the two fish, he looked up to heaven and said a blessing over them. Then he broke the loaves and gave them to the disciples to set before the crowd. 17 And they all ate and were satisfied. And what was left over was picked up, twelve baskets of broken pieces.18 Now it happened that as he was praying alone, the disciples were with him. And he asked them, "Who do the crowds say that I am?" 19 And they answered, "John the Baptist. But others say, Elijah, and others, that one of the prophets of old has risen." 20 Then he said to them, "But who do you say that I am?" And Peter answered, "The Christ of God."

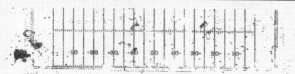

Rk	Date	Opponent	Result	Passing					Rushing				Total Offense				First Downs			Penalties		Turnovers		
				Cmp	Att	Pct	Yds	TD	Att	Yds	Avg	TD	Plays	Yds	Avg	Pass	Rush	Pen	Tot	No.	Yds	Fum	Int	Tot
12	11/27/21	@ Georgia Tech	W (45-0)	14	20	70	255	4	30	209	7	2	50	464	9.3	10	9	2	21	0	0	0	0	0

BOBBY DODD STADIUM

W 45-0

GAME TIME: 12:00 P.M. EST
GAME ATTENDANCE: 52,806

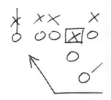

CHAPTER 13

GRATITUDE

ATLANTA, GA
DECEMBER 4, 2021

1 Make a joyful noise to the Lord, all the earth! 2 Serve the Lord with gladness! Come into his presence with singing! 3 Know that the Lord, he is God! It is he who made us, and we are his; we are his people, and the sheep of his pasture. 4 Enter his gates with thanksgiving and his courts with praise! Give thanks to him; bless his name! 5 For the Lord is good; his steadfast love endures forever, and his faithfulness to all generations.
Psalm 100:1-5

There is a story told of a blind boy who was sitting outside on some steps of a building. The boy had a hat by his feet. He held up a sign, which read, "I am blind. Please help." There were only a few coins in the hat until a certain man walked by. The man took a few coins from his pocket and dropped them into the hat. He then took the sign, turned it around, and wrote some words. Then he put the sign back in the boy's hand so that everyone who walked by would see the new words. Soon the hat began to fill up due to the large volume of people who were giving money to the blind boy. That afternoon the man who had changed the sign returned to see how things were.

The boy recognized his footsteps and asked, "Were you the one who changed my sign this morning? What did you write?"

The man said, "I only wrote the truth. I said what you said but in a different way. I wrote, *"Today is a beautiful day, but I cannot see it."*

Both signs spoke the truth. But the first sign simply said the boy was blind, while the second sign conveyed to everyone walking by how grateful they should be to see.

Think for a second. How grateful are you that you can see? How grateful are you that you can walk? How grateful are you that you can play a game you love? How grateful are you for the gifts that you possess and that other people would love to have?

As we prepare for the game today, I hope and pray that the thing that stands out to us is that God has been good to us, and we should be grateful to God. It's easy for us to miss this truth. We have talked about this day so much that it's easy to take it for granted. When you play in the SEC championship game 4 out of 5 years, it's super easy to be comfortable. When you have a new facility. When you can just go to the equipment window and get some new gear. When that direct deposit consistently hits. We all have so much to be grateful for, and if we are honest, it is easy for us to take the good gifts from the Lord for granted. Yes, are there some things that would change? For sure. Are there some prayers that you are waiting to be answered? Of course. But when we look at our lives, we should be grateful. When we consider where we are today, whether we are preparing to play in the SEC championship or simply being able to spend time with our family, those blessings should make us grateful.

I love the 100th Psalm because it reminds us of God's goodness and God's grace. If we are not careful the truth about God's goodness and God's grace can be hidden from us. Satan oftentimes wants to distract us. Satan wants to provide a smoke screen that hinders us from seeing clearly. Satan wants to blind us from those two truths! Satan wants the cares of life to blind us from seeing God's goodness and grace. The loss of the job, the miscarriage, the death in the family, the pain of being let down by the people we trust — these are all significant realities, but I'm praying that those things won't blind you from seeing the goodness of God.

So let me ask a couple of questions as you read this chapter. Can you clearly see that God is good and that God has given you grace (meaning God has given you more than you deserve)? Not in the past or even in the future, but right where you are today, can you see that the Lord is gracious, and can you see clearly that the Lord is good? Or have you been blinded by your unmet expectations? Can you see those truths, or have you been blinded by that season of suffering? Has the struggle to earn a starting spot or the struggles back at home in your family or in your health, blinded you from seeing God's grace and God's goodness?

Here is my hope —regardless of the pain and suffering that oftentimes are present in our lives, may we be able to identify God's grace and goodness that is present in our lives!

I believe that's the mindset that we need to possess to really appreciate the 100th Psalm. In the passage, we are given the truth that should lead us to something I call ThanksLiving. Last week we had Thanksgiving. I want to use the word ThanksLiving, because if we are not careful, we can be thankful with our lips while not being thankful with our lives. The 100th psalm reminds us that gratitude comes from a life lived, not just from our lip service.

The 100th Psalm is special because it focuses on being grateful for God. Now as we begin our study, we clearly see how to show gratitude, why to show gratitude, and when to show gratitude. First, let's consider how to show gratitude.

1. How to Show Gratitude

100:1 Make a joyful noise to the Lord, all the earth!

I'm sure that we have all heard the phrase, "doing anything for clout." Let me submit to you what is suggested in verse 1 is not for clout or for show. The psalmist says *I am so grateful for God that I want everyone to know it*. Occasionally when someone has done something special for us we find ourselves asking, "What can I do for so and so to show my appreciation?" Earlier this year, we spoke about our why. We spoke about why we do what we do. Many of you guys here spoke about wanting to do well because of the sacrifices made by others. About how those sacrifices made on your behalf, make you want to show your gratitude by doing well and taking care of those who have been taking care of you.

What can be done to show appreciation?

It is a valid question and not always an easy one to answer. But think about it this way: if it is hard to know how to show appreciation to another human being, then how much more difficult must it be to show appreciation to God? **Some might be wondering how should we show appreciation to God.**

We cannot thank Him enough by simply giving Him something as though He needed anything from us in the first place. While on one level, that is true. God doesn't need anything from us, but God desires things from us. God does not need anything from you, so what can we do? We should do what God desires! God desires praise! While our relationship with God is personal, it should never be private.

In the movie Friday, Smokey gets hooked up with the girl, and she tells him over the phone that she looks like Janet Jackson. However, she showed up, and Smokey said she looked like Freddie Jackson instead! He saw her, and he wanted to keep it private, so he told her *don't ever, ever, ever, ever, ever come around here again*! Smokey didn't want to be associated with her, so he didn't claim her. When we are truly grateful, we will want others to know. When we care about something, we invite others to care also.

My mom is up in Illinois, and she is actually praying for you guys today. Whenever we have a chapel service, I tell her the time, and she will stop what she is doing to pray. This week she was so excited about the game. She wanted a huge UGA flag so she could hang it outside of her house. So I sent one to the house. She cares about us, and the flag invites others to care about what she cares about. When we care about something, we invite others to also care about it. When we care about our team winning, we invite others to care about our team. When we care about our accomplishments, we make noise about it by posting about it, and in doing so we invite others to care. When you got that first offer, you tweeted. When you made an All-Conference or All-American, you post about it. When you make a watch list, you post about it because you are inviting others to care about what you care about.

In the text, the psalmist cares deeply about God, and the psalmist wants others to also care deeply about God. It is a reminder of our purpose. We are created to know God, and we are created to make God known.

We want to know God more intimately, and we want to make God known more clearly. CS Lewis says just as we spontaneously celebrate what we value, we also spontaneously invite others to celebrate what we value. Is that not true whether it's our favorite artist, designer, player, or game?

When we value something, we invite others to value it also. The psalm invites us to do what we ought to do. It's a reminder of what God has already told us. It's a reminder of what we are created for. Now what happens when we don't do that? Think about a great museum with wonderful paintings. When the lights are off, the paintings don't cease to be beautiful when no one can recognize them. If a blind person walks through the museum and is unable to see the art, then it doesn't mean it is no longer beautiful. If a deaf person cannot hear the beautiful notes of a symphony, that doesn't discredit the masterpiece. The same is true when we fail to acknowledge God. When we fail to be thankful for God and when we fail to praise God, that does not mean that God ceases to be God. God is worthy of our worship even when we withhold our worship and praise. In the passage, there is an invitation for all of creation to celebrate the creator. We have a responsibility to celebrate a God that is worthy.

And the text begins with how we show gratitude, by praising God. But secondly, we dig into why we show gratitude.

2. Why We Show Gratitude

3 Know that the Lord, he is God!
It is he who made us, and we are his;
we are his people, and the sheep of his pasture.

Verse 3 invites us to know something about God. Don't miss this! The invitation isn't for Mom and Dad. The invitation isn't just for your family, teammates, or coworkers. The invitation is personal because it is for you. God wants YOU to know Him. Knowing the playbook helps you be more confident in the game. You know what to do when the ball is hiked because you know the play. You know where you're supposed to be and what you're supposed to do. And when you don't know the play, you have no clue where to go or what your assignment should be. God wants you to be confident. The more we know, the more we are confident. The more we know about God, the more we know about ourselves. All of this helps us in our gratitude. The more we know God, the more we know ourselves. As God reveals himself, we are able to know ourselves.

I need to know how to respond in life. I need to know how to be a husband or a father. I need to know how to provide. I need direction. I need strength. I need God's help. I need God's blessing. And the more I know Him, the more I know how to receive what I need from the Lord. Since God has made us and redeemed us, we can be grateful that He knows what's best for us.

3. When to Show Gratitude

5 For the Lord is good;
his steadfast love endures forever,
and his faithfulness to all generations.

When we are made aware of God's goodness and grace, the appropriate response is to be grateful. We should be grateful not simply for what God has done, but for who God is. Here is why I love the text. God has always been good, and God always will be good!

Growing up, one of my favorite movies was *Willy Wonka & the Chocolate Factory*. You have a very poor young boy who finds a golden ticket and ends up receiving the factory as a prize. When he receives the factory, he doesn't just think about himself, but he wants to use the factory to help his family. In a very real sense, when we recognize how good God has been to us, it makes us give more gratitude to God, but it also leads us to show more grace to others. Don't miss this truth, our relationship with others will be impacted positively when we have a healthy relationship with God.

PRE-GAME CHAPEL
ATLANTA, GA
SATURDAY, DECEMBER 4, 2021

GRATITUDE

1. HOW TO SHOW GRATITUDE
- While our relationship with God is personal, it should never be private.
- When we are truly grateful, we will want others to know. When we care about something we invite others to care also.

2. WHY WE SHOW GRATITUDE
- We are grateful because God is good. As God reveals Himself, we can then know ourselves.
- Since God has made us and redeemed us, we can be grateful that He knows what's best for us.

3. WHEN TO SHOW GRATITUDE
- When we are made aware of God's goodness and grace - the appropriate response is to be grateful.
- We should be grateful not simply for what God has done, but for who God is.
- God has always been good, always is good and always will be good!

PSALM 100

1 Make a joyful noise to the Lord, all the earth!
2 Serve the Lord with gladness! Come into His presence with singing! 3 Know that the Lord, He is God! It is He who made us, and we are His; we are His people, and the sheep of His pasture. 4 Enter His gates with thanksgiving and His courts with praise! Give thanks to Him; bless His name! 5 For the Lord is good; His steadfast love endures forever, and his faithfulness to all generations.

L 41-24

GAME TIME: 4:00 P.M. EST
GAME ATTENDANCE: 78,030

Rk	Date	Opponent	Result	Passing					Rushing				Total Offense			First Downs				Penalties		Turnovers		
				Cmp	Att	Pct	Yds	TD	Att	Yds	Avg	TD	Plays	Yds	Avg	Pass	Rush	Pen	Tot	No.	Yds	Fum	Int	Tot
13	12/4/21	N. Alabama	L (24-41)	29	48	60.4	340	3	30	109	3.6	0	78	449	5.8	15	10	5	30	6	45	0	2	2

MERCEDES-BENZ STADIUM

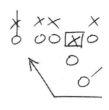

CHAPTER 14

NEXT LEVEL: HOLD THE LADDER

MIAMI GARDENS, FL
DECEMBER 31, 2021

1 Now when Sanballat and Tobiah and Geshem the Arab and the rest of our enemies heard that I had built the wall and that there was no breach left in it (although up to that time I had not set up the doors in the gates), 2 Sanballat and Geshem sent to me, saying, "Come and let us meet together at Hak-phi-rim in the plain of Ono." But they intended to do me harm. 3 And I sent messengers to them, saying, "I am doing a great work and I cannot come down. Why should the work stop while I leave it and come down to you?" 4 And they sent to me four times in this way, and I answered them in the same manner. 5 In the same way Sanballat for the fifth time sent his servant to me with an open letter in his hand. 6 In it was written, "It is reported among the nations, and Geshem also says it, that you and the Jews intend to rebel; that is why you are building the wall. And according to these reports you wish to become their king. 7 And you have also set up prophets to proclaim concerning you in Jerusalem, 'There is a king in Judah.' And now the king will hear of these reports. So now come and let us take counsel together." 8 Then I sent to him, saying, "No such things as you say have been done, for you are inventing them out of your own mind." 9 For they all wanted to frighten us, thinking, "Their hands will drop from the work, and it will not be done." But now, O God, strengthen my hands. 10 Now when I went into the house of Shemaiah the son of Delaiah, son of Mehetabel, who was confined to his home, he said, "Let us meet together in the house of God, within the temple. Let us close the doors of the temple, for they are coming to kill you. They are coming to kill you by night." 11 But I said, "Should such a man as I run away? And what man such as I could go into the temple and live? I will not go in." 12 And I understood and saw that God had not sent him, but he had pronounced the prophecy against me because Tobiah and Sanballat had hired him. 13 For this purpose he was hired, that I should be afraid and act in this way and sin, and so they could give me a bad name in

order to taunt me. 14 Remember Tobiah and Sanballat, O my God, according to these things that they did, and also the prophetess Noadiah and the rest of the prophets who wanted to make me afraid. 15 Sothe wall was finished on the twenty-fifth day of the month Elul, in fifty-two days. 16 And when all our enemies heard of it, all the nations around us were afraid and fell greatly in their own esteem, for they perceived that this work had been accomplished with the help of our God.
Nehemiah 6: 1-16

Today I want to talk to you about one of the most successful men who has ever lived. This man was not successful simply because he acquired a lot of possessions or because he accomplished his personal goal. This man was successful because he did something significant for the Lord. I want to consider his life because in looking, we see a model to follow. We see things that we can do for the rest of our lives, and we see something that we can experience for the rest of our lives. Don't miss this. When we look at his life, we see him doing one simple thing that leads to success. There is one thing in the text that he does that we can do in our lives today. Now before I tell you what it is, let me submit to you, that it wasn't simply going to chapel that made him successful. It wasn't staying out of trouble that made him successful. It wasn't feeding the hungry that made him successful. It wasn't simply meditating that made him successful. The secret to this man's success is simple. To be successful he simply stayed on the ladder.

Let me repeat that. To be successful, he stayed on the ladder. He refused to stop working until the mission was complete.

Let me explain. Chapter 6:3 simply says, "I am doing a great work and I cannot come down." Nehemiah is building a wall, and he is on top of the wall saying, "I'm not coming down until it's finished." This man refused to get off the ladder, and it led to his success. Now to appreciate Nehemiah 6, you've got to understand what took place in chapter one. In chapter 1, Nehemiah is living well. He is living in the King's palace. He is eating at the King's table. He has had a huge amount of personal success, but he wanted to go to another level. Nehemiah wasn't satisfied with his position. This man wasn't selfish; he was selfless because he was concerned about others.

In our last Skull Session (Skull Sessions are regular small group meetings where players open up about their lives and motivations), we discussed the movie *Cinderella Man.* There is a part of the movie where Russel Crowe's character explains sacrifice. In the movie, his character was to sacrifice for his daughter, and in the press conference before the big fight, he made the statement that "he was fighting for milk." We know it wasn't simply milk that was important, but it was what the milk represented that was important. In a very similar way, the Book of Nehemiah tells the story of a man rebuilding the walls of Jerusalem. The enemies of the Lord had torn apart the city, and while everything was good with Nehemiah personally, when he heard about the state of the Lord's city, he had to do something about it. When Nehemiah heard about what was going on back home, he made a decision to put in some work to rebuild the walls. Now I want you to catch this. It's not that the wall was so important. It was what the wall represented that was important. Just like in the movie, the milk wasn't important. It was what the milk represented, in this case, feeding his family.

In the day and time when the book of Nehemiah was written, the walls of the city guaranteed the protection of the city. In those days when the enemy army would pull up, there wasn't any "cappin' or "talking". When they pulled up, somebody was going to die. So, the city walls were important because the walls protected the people. Nehemiah wanted to rebuild the wall because he understood the importance of protecting the people.

So, in chapter 1, Nehemiah leaves a great job. He leaves a great palace. He leaves what is comfortable to go and rebuild the wall because the wall was important to God. Don't miss the truth, what was important to God became important to him, so he left a place where he was comfortable, and he got comfortable being uncomfortable. Nehemiah had experienced some level of success. He had done great things, but he wanted to go to another level. He wanted to do something that would bless his people. In chapter 6, the wall is almost complete, but there is still work left to do. He had experienced quite a few victories. The people in his community were singing his praises, but he hadn't reached his ultimate goal. He hadn't accomplished the mission. He is close. He is almost finished with what he had started. He is close. He is working on the ladder, but as soon as he gets too close to completing the mission, he is presented with a great distraction.

1. Next Level: Be Prepared for a Great Distraction (vv. 1-2).

2 Sanballat and Geshem sent to me, saying, "Come and let us meet together at Hakkephirim in the plain of Ono." But they intended to do me harm. 3 And I sent messengers to them, saying, "I am doing a great work and I cannot come down. Why should the work stop while I leave it and come down to you?"

I want to submit to you many times in life when Satan cannot defeat us, the next best option is to distract us. He knows that the project is almost complete. The enemies of the project attempt to distract Nehemiah from the work. As we read the passage, I believe we would do well to consider how we are handling the distractions that are presented to us. Here is the truth: we will all deal with distractions — the question is, how are we dealing with those distractions?

When Nehemiah responds, we see a response rooted and grounded in humility. Nehemiah was humble enough to evaluate his work. He was humble enough to assess what work had been done. Let me ask you a question. When people come to you, are you honest enough to make a sober assessment of what has been accomplished? Or are you so prideful that you are unwilling to operate in the truth? Nehemiah was humble enough to evaluate his progress, but he was also honest. He wasn't so prideful and puffed up that he couldn't be honest. He wasn't so defensive that he couldn't admit that while there were no breaks in the wall, the gates needed to be installed. The gates needing to be installed meant there were significant areas that needed to be addressed. He wasn't so big-headed and boastful that he tried to over-exaggerate the work that had been done.

Nehemiah's response reveals his humility and that he operated with integrity. But as you continue to read, we see that he is still hungry. He didn't allow the success that he experienced to allow him to hit cruise control. He didn't allow the victories in the past to allow him to think that he had arrived. Nehemiah was so focused on finishing the mission that he did not get caught up in the distractions. We all need what

Nehemiah possessed: humility, honesty, and hunger. We need the ability to see our good progress without neglecting the work that remains. As believers, we need to learn how to live balancing God's rest and God's work. Eternally, we must learn to rest in the finished work that Christ accomplished on the cross, knowing that our salvation is secure. We know that our salvation is secure because salvation is not based upon our performance, but based solely upon what Christ performed on our behalf. And while we rest in the finished work of Christ, that doesn't give us a license to be lazy. Furthermore, it should never serve as an excuse to not show my genuine faith in Christ by performing works that honor Christ.

When we read Nehemiah's words here, we should be reminded we will never reach a day on this side of glory when we have done all there is to do. Yes, we need to affirm the progress. Nehemiah specifically mentioned the progress, but he is not satisfied with the progress. Especially when there is so much more progress that we can make. Let me practically apply this principle. Yes, my marriage may have experienced a lot of progress, but what work is there left to do? Yes, my relationship with my children is growing, but what work is there left to do? Yes, I have joined a local church, and I go more often than I used to, but think for a moment, what work is left to do?

In my marriage, I don't simply want to survive and stay married, but by God's grace, I want to thrive. With my kids, I don't simply want to keep a roof over their heads, but I want to have a growing relationship that is marked by trust, accountability, and encouragement. I don't simply want to warm up a pew at church, but I want to use my gifts, time, talent, and treasure for the building of God's kingdom!

I believe we would all do well to read this chapter to humble ourselves and evaluate where we are with Christ and what we have accomplished for Christ. And as we humbly assess our progress, I hope we can be honest about that progress. Nehemiah didn't take the attitude that he was fine having accomplished more in 52 days than his father and brother accomplished in 52 years. He still wanted to do more. And no matter how much progress we have made, I pray that we will be hungry for more progress, knowing that God desires to use us all at a greater level. Coming to church is great, but how can you continue to progress? Being married is great, but how can you continue to progress?

To have success on the next level you have to be able to deal with great distractions.

But to have greater success on the next level, you must possess great determination.

2. Next Level: Possess Great Determination.

When we hear a story about a man building a wall, it is easy for us to wonder what is so great about finishing a wall. What is so great about hanging doors on a gate? Let me say something here. Any work is great work if that is the work God has called you to do. Let me say it another way. Every work God calls you to do is a great work in His eyes. Doesn't matter your role on the team, family, or company, God can do great things in you and through you. If you were getting ready to play a game today, the fact that you are on the team, means you are significant. You might not carry the ball, or throw the ball or even touch the field, but whatever role you are called to play is a great role because of God's calling you to that role.

Months earlier, Nehemiah was living in a palace, and now he is living on a work site. Please know this, though, that the work site is significant. Months earlier, he was having conversations with the king, and now he is having conversations with refugees, but please know what he was doing was significant. Months earlier, he was eating at the King's table, but now he is sharing food rations. Please know what he was doing is significant. We need to remember that whatever we do for God is significant. The work Nehemiah was doing in Jerusalem was not great because the world said that it was significant. The world would have called what he was doing in Persia significant, but there is nothing more significant than doing what God has called you to do!

Let me ask you a question: what are you currently doing in your life that God would consider significant? Not the world. Not your colleagues. Not even your parents, Facebook friends, or Instagram followers. But God. Please hear this. Significance is less about the work you do and more about why you are working and who you are working for! Nehemiah could not leave for the meeting because leaving meant he would be leaving God's will and God's work. Nehemiah says, "*I can't come down the ladder because I am doing a great work.*" Nehemiah's life reminds us that we should never settle for something good when God wants us to do something greater. We must make the commitment to never leave God's will and never put down God's work

As believers, we must be prepared for Satan to tempt us to delay God's work, but also to distract us from God's work as well! People may ask us to do something good, but the question I must ask myself is, *Is this God's will?* It might seem like a minor break skipping a class, or workout, academic appointment, or church. That all might seem small, but we must continue doing what God has called us to do in every area of our lives.

The verse continues by saying,

9 For they all wanted to frighten us, thinking, "Their hands will drop from the work, and it will not be done." But now, O God, strengthen my hands.

Nehemiah responds *Lord, strengthen my hands.* You usually don't pray for strength unless you are losing it. And if you're not losing it, you at least, must understand how much you need it! What areas of your life do you need the Lord to strengthen your hands? In your marriage? In your sexual life? In the area of pride? On your job? In your fears? Amid your failures? In the text, they were putting pressure on him to walk away from a standard, but Nehemiah prays that the Lord will allow him to be strong in the midst of the discouragement. Stay faithful to who you are! Always remember that any work is a great work if that is the work God has called you to do. No matter what was said about him Nehemiah remembered who had called, chosen, and equipped him for the work.

To have success on the next level, we must handle distractions. We must possess determination.

And lastly, we need discernment.

3. Next Level: Practice Great Discernment (vv. 10-14).

I'll close with this. I've shared this passage before, and usually, when I preach on Nehemiah, I'm focused on the man. I like to focus on how he was on top of the ladder, and he was unwilling to come down. We all know that the purpose of a ladder is to go from one level to the next. But if you have ever been on a ladder, you know that the higher you go on the ladder, the more important it is to have someone holding the ladder.

In life, it is so easy to see who is on the top of the ladder, but here is what I love about a team. We get to accomplish more together than we ever would separately! And for us to go higher, we're going to need guys to hold the ladder. Now a lot of times, we get caught up with who is at the top of the ladder, but I want to submit to you the person at the bottom of the ladder is just as important as the one at the top. I really believe the one at the bottom of the ladder is *MORE* important. Today I want to encourage you to hold on to the ladder. That's what it is going to take. We need guys to hold the ladder. Pride can distract you from holding the latter. Selfishness can keep you from holding the latter. Your attitude can keep you from holding the latter.

But fully trusting in the Lord will help you operate in humility. And it is that humility that should lead you to HOLD THE LADDER!

GAME FOURTEEN
DEVOTIONAL CARD

PRE-GAME CHAPEL
MIAMI GARDENS, FL
FRIDAY, DECEMBER 31, 2021

NEXT LEVEL: HOLD THE LADDER

1. To have success on the next level we must be prepared for a great **distraction**. (vv. 1-2)
   - Stay focused on where you are going!
   - Though Nehemiah was presented with a distraction, his life displays humility, honesty & hunger.
   - Nehemiah made a commitment to complete what he started - because what he started was too important not to complete.

2. To have success on the next level we must possess great **determination**. (vv. 3-9)
   - Stay faithful to who you are!
   - Always remember that any work is a great work, if it is the work that God has called you to do.
   - No matter what was said about him, Nehemiah remembered who had called, chose & equipped him for the work.

3. To have success on the next level we must practice great **discernment**. (vv. 10-14)
   - Stay firm in what you believe!
   - In life we will hear several voices, but there is really only one voice that matters most!
   - We must resist the urge to get off the ladder. We must also resist the urge to reject holding the ladder. To go higher we must accept that holding the ladder is just as important as being on top of the ladder.

Nehemiah 6

1 Now when Sanballat and Tobiah and Geshem the Arab and the rest of our enemies heard that I had built the wall and that there was no breach left in it (although up to that time I had not set up the doors in the gates), 2 Sanballat and Geshem sent to me, saying, "Come and let us meet together at Hakkephirim in the plain of Ono." But they intended to do me harm. 3 And I sent messengers to them, saying, "I am doing a great work and I cannot come down. Why should the work stop while I leave it and come down to you?" 4 And they sent to me four times in this way, and I answered them in the same manner. 5 In the same way Sanballat for the fifth time sent his servant to me with an open letter in his hand. 6 In it was written, "It is reported among the nations, and Geshem also says it, that you and the Jews intend to rebel; that is why you are building the wall. And according to these reports you wish to become their king. 7 And you have also set up prophets to proclaim concerning you in Jerusalem, 'There is a king in Judah.' And now the king will hear of these reports. So now come and let us take counsel together." 8 Then I sent to him, saying, "No such things as you say have been done, for you are inventing them out of your own mind." 9 For they all wanted to frighten us, thinking, 'Their hands will drop from the work, and it will not be done." But now, O God, strengthen my hands. 10 Now when I went into the house of Shemaiah the son of Delaiah, son of Mehetabel, who was confined to his home, he said, "Let us meet together in the house of God, within the temple. Let us close the doors of the temple, for they are coming to kill you. They are coming to kill you by night." 11 But I said, "Should such a man as I run away? And what man such as I could go into the temple and live? I will not go in." 12 And I understood and saw that God had not sent him, but he had pronounced the prophecy against me because Tobiah and Sanballat had hired him. 13 For this purpose he was hired, that I should be afraid and act in this way and sin, and so they could give me a bad name in order to taunt me. 14 Remember Tobiah and Sanballat, O my God, according to these things that they did, and also the prophetess Noadiah and the rest of the prophets who wanted to make me afraid. 15 So the wall was finished on the twenty-fifth day of the month Elul, in fifty-two days. 16 And when all our enemies heard of it, all the nations around us were afraid and fell greatly in their own esteem, for they perceived that this work had been accomplished with the help of our God.

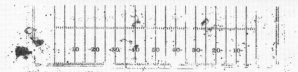

W 34-11
GAME TIME: 7:30 P.M. EST
GAME ATTENDANCE: 66,839

Rk	Date	Opponent	Result	Passing					Rushing			Total Offense			First Downs				Penalties		Turnovers		
				Comp	Att	Pct	Yds	TD	Att	Avg	TD	Plays	Yds	Avg	Pass	Rush	Pen	Tot	No.	Yds	Fum	Int	Tot
14	12/31/21	N. Michigan*	W (34-11)	21	31	67.7	331	4	35	190	5.4	0	66	521	7.9	9	12	0	21	5	70	0	0	0

HARD ROCK STADIUM

CHAPTER 15
BEAT AS ONE

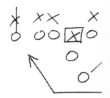

INDIANAPOLIS, IN
JANUARY 10, 2022

20 "I do not ask for these only but also for those who will believe in me through their word 21 that they may all be one just as you, Father, are in me, and I in you, that they also may be in us so that the world may believe that you have sent me. 22 The glory that you have given me I have given to them that they may be one even as we are one, 23 I in them and you in me, that they may become perfectly one so that the world may know that you sent me and loved them even as you loved me. 24 Father, I desire that they also whom you have given me may be with me where I am to see the glory that you have given me because you loved me before the foundation of the world. 25 O righteous Father even though the world does not know you I know you and these know that you have sent me. 26 I made known to them your name and I will continue to make it known that the love with which you have loved me may be in them, and I in them."
John 17: 20-26

Many of us are familiar with the Make-A-Wish Foundation. The storied nonprofit has a well-known reputation for creating life-changing experiences for children battling critical diseases. Essentially, the organization grants one extravagant request for an unforgettable experience for the child. And while many of the kids have gone on to live long lives after the request was granted, there are quite a few that pass away, unfortunately, soon after.

Think for a second: what if you were granted one wish?

Say you were the one dealing with a terminal illness and were able to make just one request. What would that be? I know you're young. I know you're strong. I know you've got a lot of life ahead of you. But what if you were facing the end, and you could only make one final request? What would it be?

Would it be for a win?

Would it be for a big contract?

Would it be something for your family?

Think hard.

What would it be?

Unsure? That's understandable. Maybe you don't know exactly what your request would be. But I can guarantee that whatever it is, it would be important. If you had a grave sickness and were knocking on death's door, then the thing you would ask for would be something of immense significance. It would be near and dear to your heart. Now, if we can appreciate the importance of such a wish, we should understand the gravity of Jesus's prayer request in John 17.

In the text, Jesus is about to die. He's going to the cross. He's about to face an unjust, brutal, and despicable death. He's about to take our place and die for our sins. This is the last time all of the disciples would be together. Kind of like this is the last game where we'll all be together. And knowing this fact — that this would be the last time they were all in one place, sharing space with one another, Jesus makes a final request.

He makes a wish.

He tells them what is most important.

He tells them what is near and dear to his heart.

Jesus doesn't ask for a new house or a car. Jesus doesn't wish to throw out the first pitch at the World Series or to be team captain for the game. Jesus doesn't even make an appeal that we go to church or that we write a big check for the church's benefit. Jesus's last request is clear and powerful.

Jesus requests simply that we Beat as One.

Think about the one thing you want more than anything else. In John 17, the thing that Jesus wanted, more so than anything else, is that we become one. He says the world will know that you are with me because of how you love one another.

It's not unlike trademarks. The greatest designers and manufacturers around the world have a trademark or logo registered for their products. Apple has a distinct logo. Amazon has a distinct logo. Coca-Cola has a distinct logo. Gucci has a distinct logo. Whether it's Nike, Prada, Bentley, Ferrari, or Louis Vuitton, they all have built a unique brand with a memorable logo. At a grocery store, you know what to expect on the inside of a box because of what is emblazoned on the outside of the box. The very things that are on the outside identify what is on the inside. The same can be said for human beings. Everyone reading this right now has a unique identifier on the outside. It's called a fingerprint.

Your fingerprint, much like a company trademark, is the unique identifier in your life. When I consider the text of John 17, we should be reminded that God has a trademark for which He wishes to be known. It's an identifier that lets the world know who He is and who belongs to Him. Believe it or not, that identifier is love.

How we love another is our emblazoned mark. It's our identifier. Beating as one and loving one another is something that God wants to serve as His logo, His trademark, and His identifier. That is why this game has presented one of the greatest opportunities ever. Do we simply want to be known for wearing the G for UGA? Do we want to be famous for being from the SEC? Or for our school being located in Athens? Or do we want to be known for being together?

If we were to look ahead in the text to John 18, we'd see that Jesus is arrested right after he finishes his prayer. On the night of John 17, Jesus is praying...praying that all disciples would be unified.

Don't miss that.

Jesus doesn't pray that we have more money, more wins, or more influence. He's not interested in those things. Those aren't his chief concerns.

To be more specific, Jesus doesn't even pray for uniformity. He doesn't want us to be the same. He knows His disciples are different. In fact, that's one of the very things that Christ loves most about them. Jesus prays for unity. He prays that we are one in spirit and purpose. Christ prays for the unity of all believers!

In our last chapter, I simply stated that when Satan cannot defeat us, he will oftentimes, try to distract us. Therefore, we need to hold the ladder. We need to make sure we don't get distracted. This week, we want to consider the reality that when Satan is unsuccessful in distracting us, then Satan will try to divide us!

As we transition to our passage, it is clear to see that beating as one is based upon a message.

1. The Message (v.20)

20 "I do not ask for these only, but also for those who will believe in me through their word

The unity that Jesus is praying for is based on a message. A logical next question should be if *beating as one* is based upon a message, then what was the message? Good question. It is the Gospel message. Simply put, God loves us, and God cares for us. And to take it a step further, God's love for us does not change based on the scoreboard, the draft order, or the title we possess. The message is that we are more sinful than we would like to admit but more loved than we can imagine. The message is that God so loved the world that he came to die for our sins in our place.

The message that brings unity is the Gospel message, and it's based upon the truth and can never be given at the expense of the truth. The message that we have received this year is 1 + 1= 3. We have accepted the message that we are better together. Our focus should not be on creating unity, but rather our focus should be on keeping it!

Beating as one is based on the message, and beating as one is based upon the right motivation.

2. The Motivation

23 I in them and you in me that they may become perfectly one so that the world may know that you sent me and loved them even as you loved me.

Beating as one is vital because beating as one is God's best. Beating as one is important because it keeps us strong. In life, we must accept that the more you divide something, the weaker it gets. Let's take a quick trip to the movies. In the film *American Gangster*, Denzel Washington's character, Frank Lucas, had to have an intense talk with drug dealer Nicky Barnes. Frank had built an empire selling cocaine branded "Blue Magic." Nicky, trying to make a little extra money, was cutting and diluting it. The more he divided Blue Magic, the weaker it became. It lost its effect. It lost its potency and impact. Nicky Barnes was ruining the reputation and name of Blue Magic. Beating as one keeps us strong. It keeps us pure, potent, and impactful. It protects us from being weak.

Never thought you'd learn about the dope game in a devotional message, huh?

Read verse 23 with me again.

23 I in them and you in me, that they may become perfectly one, so that the world may know that you sent me and loved them even as you loved me
This unity does not happen automatically or easily. It must be worked at. It takes hard work and can be easily destroyed.

Today we are playing in Lucas Oil Stadium, but I am old enough to remember the RCA Dome. When the RCA dome was built, it took two years to complete. Once it was finished, it was the largest dome in the world. It took 2 years and over $100 million to construct the dome. However, when Lucas Oil Stadium opened up, the RCA dome was torn down. Architects and structural engineers strategically placed explosives throughout the dome structure. They put together a plan that focused on taking out the load-bearing pillars, and although it took 2 years to build, it was destroyed in a matter of only seconds. It takes time to build unity on a team, in a community, or in a family. But Satan tries to strategically place explosives that lead to division and destruction. When you don't get to start. When you don't get the reps. When you don't win the awards. When you don't get your way. Satan can use those things to destroy our unity, and that is why Jesus prayed that we beat as one!

Beating as one is based upon a message.

Beating as one is based on a specific motivation.

And lastly, beating as one is a divine mandate.

3. The Mandate

24 Father, I desire that they also, whom you have given me, may be with me where I am, to see my glory that you have given me because you loved me before the foundation of the world.

Verse 24 reveals his desire. Jesus wants us. He wants us to be where He is. He desires that we be with Him, but also that we see Him as He truly is. Jesus wants us to see His deity by seeing His glory. Many of us have seen the show Undercover Boss, where a president or CEO of a Fortune 500 company becomes an employee of their company. They take off their fine clothes and leave the corner office. They humble themselves and drive to work themselves instead of being chauffeured. Rather than calling the shots, the CEO serves those who should be serving him. That CEO gets to know the employees and workers in close proximity by working alongside and for them. At the end of the show, the President in disguise takes off the prosthetics and reveals their true identity and status. If we can understand the dynamics that take place on a show like *Undercover Boss*, then maybe we'll get a glimpse of what

Jesus is alluding to here. He wants us to see His glory and His true character.

25 O righteous Father, even though the world does not know you, I know you, and these know that you have sent me. 26 I made known to them your name, and I will continue to make it known, that the love with which you have loved me may be in them, and I in them."

Jesus closes his prayer with a vow to the Father, but that's not all it is...it's also a promise to us. He will continue to make His name (meaning all that He is) known to us, but He will also be increasing the Father's love in us. That is His sovereign vow, and it will be our continuing experience. Blessed be His name! What a glorious promise!

Some will experience more of this in this life than others. Why? They clearly see the passion of Christ's earthly prayer for his church and perceive their duty to draw near to Him, feed on His Word, and humbly serve one another. May we all be part of the answer to our Savior's prayer!

Let me close with this story:

A man became lost while driving through the country. As he tried to read a map, he accidentally drove off the road into a ditch. Though he wasn't injured, his car was stuck deep in the mud. Seeing a farmhouse just down the road, the man walked over to ask for help from the farmer on the property.

The farmer pointed to an old mule and said, "Warwick can get you out of the ditch."

The man took a hard look at the old mule. Then he looked back at the farmer. Knowingly, the farmer nodded reassuringly, "Yep, old Warwick can do the job." The man figured he had nothing to lose, so the two men and Warwick made their way back to the ditch. After the farmer hitched the old mule to the car and snapped the reins, he shouted, "Pull, Fred! Pull, Jack! Pull, Ted! Pull, Warwick!" And with what appeared to be very little effort, that lone mule hoisted the car from the ditch. The man was amazed! He thanked the farmer profusely and patted the mule, asking, "That was incredible! Wow! But why did you call out all those other names before you called Warwick?"

The farmer grinned and said, "Well, old Warwick is just about blind as a bat, but as long as he believes he's part of a team, he doesn't mind pulling."

It's so amazing to be a part of God's team, isn't it?

Brothers and sisters, I am so thankful to be a part of this team. I'm grateful we're here together, sharing this space one more time. And I want to challenge you to take some time, before we leave the hotel, to tell someone why you are thankful they are on this team. If you're just reading this devotional on your own or with your group, take some time to tell them why you're thankful they are on God's team. Hug your spouse, your family, your friends. Let them know how grateful you are for them. Let's commit to beat as one, not just today but for every day of our lives moving forward.

Because we're only going to go as far as we go, together. And we're better together!

DEVOTIONAL
INDIANAPOLIS, IN
MONDAY, JANUARY 10, 2022

BEAT AS ONE

1. THE MESSAGE
- The message that helps us "Beat as One" is the Gospel message.
- Belief in the message of Gospel leads to a blessing because it based on truth!
- Our focus should not simply be on creating unity, but in keeping unity!
- The truth is, we are better together! For our team: **1 + 1 = 3.**

2. THE MOTIVATION
- "Beating as One" is important because beating as one is God's best.
- "Beating as One" is our witness to world.
- This unity does not happen automatically or easily – it takes work!

3. THE MANDATE
- "Beating as One" is not simply a suggestion it is a command!
- Jesus desires to be close to us - but he also desires that we be close to one another!
- "Beating as One" shows the world the love God and brings Glory to God!

JOHN 17

20 "I do not ask for these only, but also for those who will believe in me through their word, 21 that they may all be one, just as you, Father, are in me, and I in you, that they also may be in us, so that the world may believe that you have sent me. 22 The glory that you have given me I have given to them, that they may be one even as we are one, 23 I in them and you in me, that they may become perfectly one, so that the world may know that you sent me and loved them even as you loved me. 24 Father, I desire that they also, whom you have given me, may be with me where I am, to see my glory that you have given me because you loved me before the foundation of the world. 25 O righteous Father, even though the world does not know you, I know you, and these know that you have sent me. 26 I made known to them your name, and I will continue to make it known, that the love with which you have loved me may be in them, and I in them."

LUCAS OIL STADIUM

Rk	Date	Opponent	Result	Passing					Rushing				Total Offense		First Downs				Penalties		Turnovers		
				Cmp	Att	Pct	Yds	TD	Att	Yds	Avg	TD	Plays	Yds	Avg	Pass	Rush	Pen	Tot	No.	Yds	Fum	Int	Tot
15	1/10/72 N	Alabama*	W (33-18)	17	26	65.4	224	2	30	140	4.7	1	56	364	6.5	10	7	3	20	10	70	1	0	1

W 33-18

GAME TIME: 8:00 P.M. EST
GAME ATTENDANCE: 68,311

Made in the USA
Columbia, SC
06 February 2024